EVERYDAY
STOICISM

For Ollie and Lola
the worst rock-paper-scissors players
in the world
ever

EVERYDAY STOICISM

ANCIENT SOLUTIONS TO MODERN-DAY PROBLEMS
FROM MARCUS AURELIUS AND THE STOICS

GARETH SOUTHWELL

greenfinch

CONTENTS

INTRODUCTION

Where do you go when you have problems? Well, it will depend. For leaking pipes, you call a plumber; for a faulty starter motor, a car mechanic. If you have a toothache, you visit a dentist; a cricked back, a chiropractor. But what if your problems are of a more personal nature? You're feeling stressed at work, your marriage is in crisis, you're drinking too much or you feel unaccountably depressed. Who do you visit then? A doctor? A therapist? A priest?

Whoever you choose, probably bottom of your list (if they even make it) is a philosopher. Perhaps you think modern philosophy just too obscure, involving pure (and seemingly pointless) theorizing, and focusing on the sorts of 'deep' questions from which few of us could benefit, even if we knew the answers – and often, there don't seem to be any. But whether this reputation is justified or not, it certainly hasn't always been this way.

Stoicism was a school of philosophy that began in ancient Greece sometime around 300 BC. It gets its name from the Stoa Poikile (Greek for 'painted porch'), which was a decorated colonnade near the Agora (public square) in Athens where the early Stoics would gather to discuss philosophy. It eventually spread to Rome, where, adopted by everyone from slaves to emperors, it came to dominate the cultural outlook, rising almost to the status of an unofficial state religion. From there, it would influence the development of Christianity and, through the rediscovery of classical literature and ideas during the Renaissance, go on to shape the modern Western educational curriculum, as the young minds of future politicians and writers, from Shakespeare to Churchill, were drilled on the Stoic exploits of Cato the Younger and Marcus Aurelius. As a result, even if philosopher doesn't make your list, it's not unlikely that the therapist has read their Epictetus and will encourage you to let go of those things that are out of your control; or that the priest, drawing on Seneca, will counsel you to place your trust in Providence and have faith that God has ordered the world for the best.

The five hundred or so years in which Stoicism flourished was a period of vibrant intellectual inquiry. To give things a little context, the founder of Stoicism – Zeno of Citium (334–262 BC) – is said to have come to Athens in around 312 BC. This was some ten years after the death of Aristotle (384–322 BC) and thirty-five after that of Plato (427–347 BC) – two of the biggest names in philosophy ever since and whose respective schools were still then thriving. The young Zeno would also have been exposed to the views of the Cynics, a school whose most famous adherent, Diogenes of Sinope (*c.*403–*c.*324 BC), attempted to strip life back to its essentials by living in self-imposed poverty, owning practically nothing and living in a barrel (a reaction, perhaps, against his previous profession as a banker). There was also the Megarian school, which propounded an ethical philosophy based on the ideas of Plato's teacher Socrates (469–399 BC); the Dialectical school, which focused on logic and argument; the Cyrenaics, which professed a form of sensual hedonism as the path to a happy life – and various others.

We will look at some of these competing approaches later on as we explore how that of Stoicism differs; the main point here is that Stoic philosophy did not grow up in isolation, but was influenced and challenged by contemporary philosophical schools and outlooks. Zeno himself began as a Cynic, before switching to the Megarian school. Later on, developing his own ideas, he would therefore have been well versed in the philosophical traditions that had preceded him. Ancient Athens was an intellectual melting pot, a Mecca for those who sought to imbibe philosophy at its source, and so drew students from far and wide. In fact, it is interesting to note that – Zeno himself included – all heads of the Greek Stoic school were non-Athenians. I guess the parallel today would be trainee chefs or aspiring fashion designers who make a pilgrimage to Paris.

How were the Stoics different from these other schools? Before getting into that, the first thing to note is that Stoicism – like Christianity, psychoanalysis or any cultural movement – is not a single unified thing. Over the centuries, there were developments, debates, differences of opinion and emphasis. For instance, Zeno's successor, Cleanthes (331–232 BC), emphasized the practical aspects of Stoicism and focused on relaying its central message in simple terms. In contrast, *his* successor, Chrysippus (*c.*280–*c.*206 BC), was keen to defend Stoicism against its competitors and eagerly engaged in sophisticated argument and debate regarding the finer points of Stoic doctrine. Another example: Zeno had argued that wealth, health, beauty and other such benefits were morally neutral – being rich and pretty didn't make you good (or bad). But he also thought we might still rationally prefer them over their opposites (poverty, sickness and ugliness), and therefore it was OK to pursue them as long as they didn't conflict with being virtuous. But later Stoics differed on this point. Aristo (*fl.* third century BC) argued that we should ignore *all* such benefits, focusing solely on virtue, while Panaetius (*c.*185–*c.*110 BC) went further in the other direction, arguing that there might be times when such things as wealth and health are *necessary* in order to live a truly virtuous and happy life. But, however they differed, all these thinkers are still considered Stoics, and while it is interesting here and there to note these differences, I shall instead concentrate on what they had in common. This is intended to be a practical book, something that will help you apply Stoicism's central lessons to your everyday life, so I will generally avoid the sort of academic subtleties that might otherwise bore you.

So, what did the Stoics believe? This can be summarized quite briefly. Above all, Stoicism was a practical philosophy.

Yes, Stoics held beliefs about logic, epistemology, metaphysics, ontology and other areas of philosophy; they also made interesting contributions to natural philosophy (science), philosophy of religion and what we would now call psychology. Some of these subjects will be relevant – and where they are, we will discuss them – but their main contribution, and why modern readers continue to be interested in Stoicism, is because of their views on *ethics*. This word had a slightly broader sense in ancient Greece than it does now, some of which is still retained in our use of the word 'ethos', and concerns not just morality, but also how to develop one's character and attitude to life so as to become happy and virtuous.

A Stoic believed that life was governed by Fate or Providence. As such, everything that happens is out of our control – *except* for how we *react* to what happens. So, Fortune dictates that you lose your job, your cat dies or you break your arm. Maybe you had some part to play in these events – you spent too many office hours scrolling through Facebook, you neglected your cat or decided that, yes, it was fine to cycle home after half a bottle of wine. In your defence, perhaps you could argue that Fate has also determined that you are lazy, neglectful and reckless (we'll come back to that ...). But whatever the case, what you *do* have a say in is how you *take* your cat's death/job loss/broken arm. Do you get distraught, become inconsolable? Shout and scream? Bemoan your unhappy lot? Or do you bear it ... *stoically*. Do you remind yourself that the only bit of you that is really under your control is the square foot behind your eyes, and that all other things must be accepted and wisely put up with? That death, disease and disgrace are – to anyone, anywhere, at any time – at least a possibility, and in some cases (we're all mortal, after all) inevitable? And this applies to everything in your life.

But why should you accept all of this? If the world is cruel, unfair and unfeeling, shouldn't you be doing your bit to change that? Well, of course. Stoicism doesn't suggest you shouldn't *try*; it merely points out that you should prepare yourself for when you fail – because, in all likelihood, fail you will. Maybe not now, or with this or that particular endeavour, but at some time and in some respect. And when you do, it pays to be prepared.

As well as acceptance of your own ultimate powerlessness, Stoics asked that you 'live in conformity with Nature'. By this, they did not mean organic gardening, camping or stripping off at the beach; they had in mind Nature (with a capital 'N'), by which they meant the total physical universe and the rational mind (*Logos*) that they believed inhabited and ordered it. To them, this was 'God', and as such they were *pantheists*: the idea that God was identical and inseparable from the universe. Two important things follow from this: we are all a part of God, and God controls everything that happens. As human beings, we share in God's rational nature, our minds are small puddles in the sea of his vast intellect (so to speak). And so, though we may not always understand why this or that misfortune befalls us, we must trust that it does so for a divinely ordained reason, because the world is ultimately *rational*. There is, therefore, a guiding order to existence, and by aligning ourselves with it – achieving a sort of 'flow' – we can be happy and virtuous (a similar idea to 'following Nature' can be found in Taoism and its doctrine of following the flow of the *Tao*, or 'the Way').

There is more to Stoicism than this, and both these beliefs need unpacking, but for now remember that these are the two foundations of Stoicism – acceptance of what we cannot control and living in accordance with Nature – for from them all other things spring. And they are, of course, related: if we accept misfortune, then we are in a better position to control our emotional responses to it; if we believe that everything happens for a reason, then such acceptance becomes more justified.

You have questions, I know, maybe even some objections – as do I. 'But what if I don't believe in God?' asks the atheist. 'And what about the problem of evil?' 'How can we choose to think differently about events if the mind is just a physical organ?' screams the neuroscientist. 'The brain is as much at the whim of natural forces as the body is!' OK! Calm down! I'm not saying there aren't potential difficulties with Stoic beliefs, but if you are at all familiar with philosophy, then you will know that such issues can likely be found with any belief system. I won't deny these controversies – in the following chapters, we will look at some of them – but I will focus on how (with a few tweaks, a bit of wiggling) Stoicism can still work for people who are alive today (i.e., you).

In the following chapters we will look at twelve themes that run through our lives: from the cradle to the grave, through love, work, education and health, I'll explore how the Stoics can still teach us important strategies and ways of coping. Through anecdotes and discussion, I'll also draw out key philosophical lessons from the Stoics' lives and writings, show how we can apply them through small everyday practices and exercises, and how Stoic attitudes can still be meaningful and useful.

Perhaps the best evidence for this continued relevance lies in the lives of the Stoics themselves. In adversity and suffering, as Fortune was outrageously pelting them with slings and arrows, they frequently displayed calmness and cheerfulness, courage and dignity. Furthermore, many of them lived lives not of quiet reflection, hidden away in their fusty libraries, but of committed social engagement – as soldiers, statesmen, fathers and mothers, dutiful offspring, and faithful public servants. For all their acceptance and forbearance, they were chiefly concerned not just with their own happiness, but with that of others. That such a world view persisted for half a millennium suggests there was something about the way they went about doing this that might be worth investigating, even if only to see whether – flawed, contradictory or outdated as in places it might occasionally be – there aren't still one or two things that we can learn from it.

LIFE

WHY YOU SHOULDN'T WORRY ABOUT THE THINGS YOU CAN'T CONTROL

1

It is fair to say that none of us really knows where life's path may lead us.

This may be taken as the fundamental lesson of Stoicism, and one which is well illustrated by the life of its founder. Zeno was born in Citium, in a Phoenician colony situated on the south-east coast of Cyprus at what is now the city of Larnaca. History records a number of other notable Zenos, among them an Eastern Roman emperor (AD c.425–491), another Stoic philosopher (Zeno of Tarsus, *fl.* 200 BC) and the more famous Zeno of Elea (c.495–c.430 BC), now chiefly remembered for his paradoxes involving speedy tortoises and tardy arrows. To differentiate him from these other Zenos, therefore, ours is most commonly referred to as Zeno of Citium, and occasionally by his contemporaries and other classical writers as Zeno the Phoenician. This is not to say that there is anything particularly 'Phoenician' about his philosophy; Zeno was Greek educated, and Stoic philosophy was heavily influenced by Socrates and Cynic philosophy, as well as aspects of the thought of Plato, Aristotle, Heraclitus and other Greek philosophers. Nonetheless, Zeno's Phoenician roots did play a key role in the course that his own life took – and in the founding of Stoicism itself.

During the first millennium BC, Phoenicia was a great sea-faring nation. Situated more or less where modern-day Lebanon now resides, it dominated trade and – as Citium attests – established colonies across the Mediterranean, of which Carthage was to become the most famous and powerful. So, it is unsurprising that by the time he reached adulthood, Zeno the Phoenician had become a wealthy sea-faring merchant, and perhaps would have remained in that career – had not Fate had other ideas.

Having purchased a quantity of Tyrian purple dye in Phoenicia, Zeno was on his way to Greece when he was shipwrecked near Piraeus, the chief port of Athens. From there, he made his way to the city of Athens itself, where legend has it – or at least Diogenes Laërtius's *The Lives and Opinions of Eminent Philosophers*, our main source for the details of Zeno's life – he entered a bookshop and came across a copy of Xenophon's *Memorabilia*. Xenophon (*c*.427–*c*.355 BC), like Plato, had been a pupil of Socrates, an Athenian philosopher who was sentenced to death for the alleged crimes of impiety and corrupting the city's youth.

'I now find that I made a prosperous voyage when I was wrecked.'

Zeno of Citium, quoted in Diogenes Laërtius,
The Lives and Opinions of Eminent Philosophers, VII, 260

It is often not the good times that cause us to reflect on the true meaning of life, but the bad ones. The fact that fortune doesn't always go our way can therefore be a good thing, because it can force us to re-evaluate our priorities and re-assess our goals, and even to question the very nature of our existence. A life of good fortune turns us into happy-go-lucky fools; misfortune turns us into philosophers. So, while to lose all your cargo in a shipwreck would be for most people a disaster, for Zeno it made him re-evaluate what he understood by the very idea of 'prosperity', and to forsake the pursuit of material wealth for the riches of philosophy. Such setbacks also allow us to develop resilience, courage and other valuable character traits for which we might not otherwise have the impetus. This means that what looks like a misfortune – from a different perspective – might turn out not to be.

'They say that [Zeno] was once scourging a slave whom he had detected in theft; and when he said to him, "It was fated that I should steal"; he rejoined, "Yes, and that you should be beaten."'

Zeno of Citium, quoted in Diogenes Laërtius,
The Lives and Opinions of Eminent Philosophers, VII, 268

Zeno had caught one of his slaves stealing. The slave's defence – perhaps he'd been eavesdropping on his master's lectures – was that he couldn't be blamed for something he had no control over. And since all events are pre-ordained by Nature or God, then wasn't the theft unavoidable? This illustrates one of the oldest chestnuts in philosophy: the problem of free will. If every natural event has a cause and humans are a part of Nature (as the Stoics believed), then we cannot possess free will, thus robbing us of moral responsibility – you can't blame someone for an action they had no say in. Zeno's response abides by the same logic: if the slave had no choice (in giving way to his larcenous inclinations), then nor does Zeno (in administering the fitting punishment). However, most Stoics argue that we do, in fact, have *some* freedom – the ability at least to form judgements – which in turn influences our tendencies to act (or not) on our instincts and impulses.

The *Memorabilia* presents a defence against these unjust charges, and its depiction of Socrates' courage, calmness of mind and moral integrity in the face of his impending death so impressed Zeno that he asked the bookseller where men such as these could be found. As luck would have it, at that very moment Crates of Thebes (c.365–c.285 BC), a prominent Cynic philosopher of the time, was passing by, and so the bookseller simply pointed at him and said, 'Follow that man!'

From that fateful day, Zeno would go on to become Crates' pupil, and later study under other eminent Greek philosophers. But the bookseller's may not have been the only finger pointing him towards philosophy. Another story details Zeno's visit to the Pythia, the famous oracle at Delphi. The oracle was the priestess of the Temple of Apollo, reputed to give divine advice to those who sought it, though this was often delivered in riddling form. Since she was visited regularly by the wealthy and powerful, the cynical might speculate that the ambiguity of her pronouncements was a protective strategy, a sort of prophetic get-out clause, whereby any guidance that turned out to be false or untrustworthy might be written off as misinterpretation. A famous example concerns King Croesus of Lydia (reigned c.560–546 BC), who consulted the oracle on whether he should invade Persia and was told that to do so would destroy a great empire. Being arrogant and uber-wealthy (his name still survives in the saying 'as rich as Croesus'), the king interpreted this as a military green light – not considering the possibility that the empire in question would turn out to be his own (which indeed it did).

However ambiguous or devious, the advice of the Pythia was held in great esteem, and even philosophers were known to seek it. Socrates himself had trodden the path up to her hilltop shrine, where he was told that, 'Socrates of all mortals is the wisest'. In true philosophical fashion, however, Socrates did not take this at face value, instead reasoning that, since he was pretty sure that he knew nothing, his wisdom lay in the fact that he was the only person who was *aware* of his own ignorance (thus laying the foundations for the famous Socratic method, a form of questioning that is meant to elicit another's true knowledge or ignorance: '*I* know nothing; what do *you* know?').

Regarding his own visit to the oracle, Zeno is reputed to have asked her how he might live the best life and was told that he should become 'of the same complexion as the dead'. For some reason, Zeno interpreted this puzzling recommendation to mean that he should devote himself to the study of the 'books of the ancients' (i.e., the writings of the philosophers).

Whether at the heavy-handed promptings of Fate or the subtler hints of divine prophecy, Zeno came to see his life as largely shaped by powers outside of his control. The Stoics considered all events to be the product of Fate. By this, they meant the immutable chain of cause-and-effect that links together everything within the physical world. For Stoicism, as I have said, Nature *is* God, but not in the Judaeo–Christian sense; rather, it is a rational mind or *Logos*, which they sometimes termed *Zeus*, and which animates and directs everything that happens – including, of course, the lives of human beings (we are a part of Nature too). This is perhaps one reason why Zeno seems to have taken prophecy very seriously, and why a number of later Stoics would write about it, arguing that, since the fate of the world was fixed, it is possible that there may be certain signs, dreams or omens that act as signposts to its eventual unfolding. Why shouldn't a benign creator warn us of what's coming? It won't change anything, but we can at least prepare ourselves mentally (which, for Stoicism, is what counts).

Stoics of different periods have chosen to emphasize the role of Fate in different ways. Seneca (c.4 BC–AD 65) – often called 'the Younger' to distinguish him from his father, Seneca the Elder, who was a prominent teacher of rhetoric – believed that it is *providential*, in that the forces that direct our lives often do so for the best – even when it appears that the opposite is the case. In contrast, Marcus Aurelius (AD 121–180) – at least, in certain moods – stressed just how powerless and insignificant we are in relation to the vastness of the universe, how arrogant it is of us to expect things to go our way, and foolish of us to be disappointed when they don't. But while they may have differed in how they chose to express this lack of personal control, the Stoics agreed that the wise do not curse Fate or fail to take responsibility for their situation in life; rather, they accept what happens to them and adapt accordingly. Part of this adaptation is to shift our perspective. For often what look like setbacks and troubles are, in fact, opportunities and lessons – blessings in disguise, perhaps – or at least, we can *choose* to see them in that way. A viewpoint from which, for example, a shipwreck may turn out not to be the unmitigated disaster that at first it seems to be.

'What more can the diviner see than death or danger or disease, or generally things of that kind?...Have I not within me a diviner who has told me the nature of good and of evil, and has explained to me the signs of both?'

Epictetus, *Discourses*, II, 7

Epictetus (AD c.50–c.120) was born into slavery, and it would have been understandable if this formative experience had made him bitter and resentful, or led him to the opposite of acceptance – a desire to overthrow the social order that had enslaved him. That he did not respond in either way illustrates not only his strength of mind and character, but also his deep understanding of the lesson that his enslavement taught him: we are *all* slaves to Fate and it's futile to wish otherwise. Here, like Zeno and other Stoics, Epictetus does not dismiss the advice of the fortune teller ('diviner'), but instead argues that our future happiness doesn't depend on it, for a Stoic philosopher is already prepared for whatever Fate can throw at them. In that sense, while you don't yet know the details, you already know in broad outline what the fortune teller will say: things are going to happen that are outside of your control. But the Stoic already knows what is 'good' and 'evil', and will not place their happiness in wealth, beauty, status or any other temporary and changeable things. The only correct attitude to the future is to be mentally prepared to accept whatever happens and to focus on what *is* in your control (your attitude to those events). The only wise path is acceptance.

THINK ABOUT...

As human beings, we tend to think of many of the things that happen to us as either 'good' or 'bad', but in doing so our evaluation is often partial and subjective. We are dissatisfied by our situation in life and feel hard done by. We deserve a pay rise or a promotion, we want straighter teeth, or longer and better holidays. We whine about our back pain, gripe about our in-laws or envy the new SUV of the guy next door. It's all about *us*, our needs and wants, our insecurities, and we rarely take a step back to put these things into wider perspective (will that SUV be good for the planet?) or consider whether what we desire would actually be good for us (will weeks of day-drinking at the pool-bar really benefit you?). And when 'bad' things happen, or 'good' things fail to, our habitual response is often one of surprise and a feeling of injustice. 'What have I done to deserve this?' we ask. 'Why me?'

'Well,' the Stoic would reply, 'why not?'

The universe doesn't owe you a living – or at least, not an SUV or straighter teeth. And nor, unfortunately, can it guarantee you a life devoid of grief and trouble. The loss of loved ones, disease, hardship – for the vast majority of us, at some point, such sufferings will be par for the course, and no one can avoid them completely. This doesn't mean that Fate, God or the universe has it in for you – don't take it personally. It merely means that you are not the centre of existence.

The good news is that there is something you can do about this. You just need to change the way you look

'Just as one says that Aesculapius has prescribed a course of riding for someone, or the cold bath, or walking bare-footed; so it may be said that the guiding Mind prescribes for a man, disease, or mutilation, or losses, or the like.'

Marcus Aurelius, *Meditations*, V, 8

There is, perhaps, no clearer illustration of the Stoic attitude to Fate than to see the same principle adopted by both emperor and slave. Despite the enormous power and privilege that the role of emperor brought with it, Marcus Aurelius was as aware as Epictetus that no one can escape destiny. And so, faced with illness, injury or some other misfortune, he advises that we treat it as 'medicine' prescribed by Nature ('the guiding Mind'), much as the famous healer Aesculapius might prescribe horse riding or cold baths to a sick patient, and trust that Fate has prescribed our misfortunes as 'treatment' to develop our character or to address some defect in it. Of course, we might also simply think of such misfortunes in terms of 'what does this experience teach me?'

at things. You need not believe in divine providence, nor that your unforeseen shipwreck is actually a supernatural nudge to get you to change your ways and focus on something more meaningful (though there were Stoics who thought this). But whatever force actually orders the world, the odds are that *its* priorities are not *yours*. So maybe adjust your mindset accordingly.

How much of your time is spent bemoaning things that are out of your control? Stoicism does not ask that you submit to *fatalism* – the idea that everything is pre-determined, resistance is pointless and so we must simply go with the flow. Instead, while encouraging you to set meaningful goals and work hard to achieve them, a Stoic would point out that the outcomes of your efforts are not guaranteed. The Stoic philosopher Antipater of Tarsus (died *c.*129 BC) drew a parallel with archery: all we can do is fix our aim and try to hit the target; what the wind does with the arrow is out of our hands. Therefore, maybe don't set such great store in results.

And since you and Fate may not share the same wish list, might it not be the case that 'bad' things may turn out to be 'good' for you? The promotion you missed out on may have proved a nightmare, involving longer hours and greater stress. Stoicism is not saying that we should, like *The Simpsons*' Ned Flanders or Voltaire's Dr Pangloss, view all events, no matter how horrible or tragic, through rose-tinted spectacles, convincing ourselves that 'Everything is for the best!' (even when it's not ...). But nor should we rule out that challenging situations, disappointments and troubles can have their upside. Difficulties and setbacks are an inherent part of life, and in learning how to cope with them we develop our character and grow as people. Perhaps your wonky teeth have a certain charm, and acquiring the confidence to accept your physical flaws is worth more than all the cosmetic dentistry money can buy.

But most fundamentally, Stoicism also asks you to question what your goals *are*. Have you got your priorities right? Will achieving your cherished ambitions indeed make you happy? Do you even know what happiness would look like? We will look at Stoicism's answer to that question in a later chapter (see page 68), but for the moment, before you blame God or Fate for your predicament, take a moment to analyse your expectations.

'God bears a fatherly mind towards good men, and loves them in a manly spirit. "Let them," says He, "be exercised by labours, sufferings, and losses, that so they may gather true strength." Those who are surfeited with ease break down not only with labour, but with mere motion and by their own weight. Unbroken prosperity cannot bear a single blow; but he who has waged an unceasing strife with his misfortunes has gained a thicker skin by his sufferings, yields to no disaster, and even though he fall yet fights on his knee.'

Seneca, *On Providence*, II, 6

Here Seneca argues that the apparent misfortunes that happen to us can be character building, providing a sort of moral workout for good people to improve and become even stronger. You may think of it as a sort of divine tough love, and he compares such things to the sort of punishing training undergone by athletes. This he contrasts with those made weak by a life of luxury and ease, whom 'a single blow' can lay low. We can question this idealism, of course, and the assumption that God or Nature would not impose such challenges upon those whose situation in life makes them unfit to meet them (such as children or the infirm). But the point is that if we have the mental courage, we may see life's ups and downs not as misfortunes, but as providing potential to grow and develop.

GOING FURTHER...

Since Stoicism is a practical philosophy, this section is aimed at helping you to embed some Stoical routines into your day-to-day life. But don't stress about it – it's not homework! Think of it more like a toolkit. If you find that one of these suggestions or exercises looks like it might help you with some problem or issue, then try it out; if not, feel free to ignore it.

1. Set aside some time – preferably each day – to be alone with your thoughts, even if it is only for fifteen or thirty minutes. If you can't find time for that, then perhaps that is itself something you should set aside some time to think about! Modern life is often hectic, I know, but consider the fact that Marcus Aurelius found time every day to work on his *Meditations* while running an empire and conducting a military campaign into Germany! So, you've no excuses, really. Plus, setting aside more time to process what's happening in your life will help you deal with the things that are overwhelming

you, thus creating more emotional and mental space. It's a virtuous circle.

2. Buy a notebook and try to write in it regularly. This can be about whatever you want – thinking through difficult relationships or events, analysing your character and bad habits, noting down interesting concepts, sage advice or inspirational quotes (see pages 224–229). Some people find journalling helpful when working through problems and emotional upheaval, and it can aid in uncovering harmful patterns of thought and behaviour. Whatever you use it for, try and keep it only for that – no shopping lists or reminders.

3. Think about a time when something bad happened to you. To begin with, choose an event that's not too recent, so that it's not too raw, and something that you have had time to process a little. Looking back, were there any upsides to what happened? Are you (or could you be) positively different now because of what happened then? What further lessons could you learn from it? How might you hope to react differently now?

MONEY

WHY HAVING IT ALL CAN LEAVE YOU WITH LESS

2

That money can't buy happiness is an old adage, and one with which the Stoics would have agreed.

Wealth, possessions, material comforts – all such things are 'hostages to fortune', to borrow a phrase from English philosopher Sir Francis Bacon (1561–1626). He was actually talking about wives and children, but the same general principle applies: if we make the source of our happiness external to ourselves, residing in things we have no control over, then we surrender our mental serenity to the whims of Fate. Your collection of antique Edwardian furniture, your lovingly restored 1960s Aston Martin, your cliff-top villa on the Amalfi coast – what happens to your pride and joy when damage, fire or theft come calling, not to mention acts of God ...?

Wealth is an example of what the Stoics called a 'preferred indifferent'. They were very black-and-white about morality, and considered that only virtue was 'good' and vice 'bad'. Everything else (whether lottery wins or shipwrecks) was morally neutral or 'indifferent', and we should, therefore, be indifferent to them. However, Zeno pointed out, while it's possible to be happy in spite of such things (or their lack), there were some that it was natural to *prefer*, and therefore – all other things being equal – it was also *natural* to seek them.

Together with health, status, power and other such preferred indifferents, money is often a prime candidate for what people *think* will make them happy. But does it? A rich person is as likely to be unlucky as a poor one, and while the wealthy might be able to afford better healthcare, their money might not prevent the sudden death of a loved one, the loss of some treasured item, or their accountant embezzling their fortune and running off with their spouse to some tropical country with sun-kissed beaches and no extradition treaty.

Apart from the fact that all you own could disappear one day, there is also no proven correlation between being rich and being happy. Yes, spending money and having beautiful things and experiences is pleasurable, but there are only so many cars, houses and paintings that a person can own, only so many extravagant holidays and exclusive seats at Broadway shows, and after a while it all begins to suffer from the law of diminishing returns. The things you once lived for now begin to drag; like a kid glutted on his stash of Halloween sweets, after a while your appetite starts to dull.

'I prefer the magnificent house to the beggar's bridge. Place me among magnificent furniture and all the appliances of luxury: I shall not think myself any happier because my cloak is soft, because my guests rest upon purple. Change the scene: I shall be no more miserable if my weary head rests upon a bundle of hay.'

Seneca, *On a Happy Life*, 25, 1

Serving under Nero, Seneca amassed a great deal of wealth and became the subject of attacks from those who thought he had profited immorally from his position. Defending himself, he argued that being rich brought with it a duty to use that wealth for good, providing greater opportunity for doing so. He also argued that money made no difference to the inner person. True, he said, he would prefer to live a life of comfort, surrounded by fine things, but while part of him 'preferred' luxury and riches, he was ultimately 'indifferent' to them. Rich or poor, he would be happy.

'Remember that you must behave as at a banquet. Is anything brought round to you? Put out your hand and take a moderate share. Does it pass by you? Do not stop it. Is it not yet come? Do not yearn in desire towards it, but wait till it reaches you. So with regard to children, wife, office, riches; and you will some time or other be worthy to feast with the gods.'

Epictetus, *Enchiridion*, XV

For Epictetus, the correct attitude to all the things we value in life – people, possessions, pleasures – is simply to enjoy them for what they are. Do not go out of your way to find them, and once found, do not try to hold on to them. They will come and go as Fate dictates, and you will be happiest if you shape your thoughts and feelings to fit that inevitability.

For evidence of this we need only consult the salacious lives of the Roman emperors (the non-Stoical ones, that is!), whose untrammelled authority led to all sorts of excesses, as each vied to outdo his predecessor in extravagance and luxury. Consider Nero (AD 37–68), who built himself a Golden House (as it became known), an enormous palace that contained walls plated with gold and polished marble, a famously revolving dining room, and hidden pipes and compartments that would shower guests with perfumes and flower petals. Elagabalus (AD c.204–222) had mountains of snow shipped into his summer gardens to mitigate the Roman heat, fed his dogs on *foie gras* and never wore the same shoes twice. There is no evidence, however, that the wealth and power that could achieve any of these luxuries made these men happy – in fact, judging by the type of people they were said to have been, the outcome seems to have been the opposite.

Which brings us to the other danger of wealth: it gives you unrivalled opportunity to be bad. Roman history is not short of examples here, either, as many emperors utilized their access to absolute power to become deranged and depraved psychopaths. Caligula (AD 12–41) turned part of his palace into a brothel, where the wives and daughters of senators and other noblemen were forced to serve as prostitutes. Aside from having his own mother murdered, Nero took to roaming the streets of Rome at night incognito, attacking and murdering random strangers. Tiberius (42 BC– AD 37) retreated to the island of Capri, where he amused himself with diverse forms of sexual cruelty, child abuse and general depravity.

For such reasons, the Stoics argued that we should not base our happiness on wealth. They were influenced in this by the Cynics – Zeno, you may recall, first apprenticed himself to Crates, a leading Cynic of the time, and this obviously made a deep impression on him. The most famous exponent of Cynicism was Diogenes of Sinope, who by word and example advocated a life of extreme simplicity and 'naturalness'. As mentioned in the introduction (see page 8), he famously lived in a barrel – albeit a large one, turned on its side to provide shelter – possessing only a cloak for warmth and a bowl for food and water. One story relates how he even got rid of the bowl, when one day he noticed a child drinking from a fountain using only his cupped hands. By living as simply as possible, Diogenes sought to show that happiness is not reliant on wealth or possessions. Instead, he emphasized that a good, happy life can be maintained by living in accordance with Nature and displaying no embarrassment about the natural functions that we share with the animals (there are stories of him defecating and masturbating in public quite unselfconsciously!). For this animal-like authenticity, the Cynics were therefore known as 'dogs' ('cynic' comes from the Greek *kunikós*, meaning 'dog-like').

However, Zeno eventually moved on from his Cynic tutor, and one reason for this is perhaps that, while he agreed that money could not buy happiness, there was also no reason to deprive oneself of it needlessly. Being poor in itself does not make you virtuous or happy, and there are actually situations where money can help us to do good (such as to relieve the suffering of others by giving to charitable causes). There are even some stories that suggest that Zeno did not lose his fortune on that fateful shipwreck, and that he arrived in Athens a wealthy man. And while it is true that some Stoics were poor – such as Zeno's successor Cleanthes, who had to work at night to support himself, and Epictetus, who was born into slavery – others, such as Seneca, were extremely wealthy. And let's not forget Marcus Aurelius, of course, who as emperor was not short of a penny or two.

Some Stoics went further than Zeno, arguing that not only did wealth make it easier to do good, but also that the principles of commerce did not always have to square with those of morality. For instance, Diogenes of Babylon (c.230–c.150 BC) argued that as long as one's goods are not defective, stolen, or whatever, then a seller has no duty to disclose all relevant facts. Let's say that you own a shop that sells gaming and computer equipment. You have a large stock of a new games console of which there is currently a market shortage due to a production problem, and which you are, therefore, able to sell at a higher-than-normal price. However, due to insider knowledge, you also know that the production issue will soon be resolved, which will flood the market with consoles, driving down the inflated price of your stock. Do you have a duty to let your buyers know this? Diogenes argued that you do not, because getting the best price for your goods is part of running your business well. If you disclosed everything you knew – such as the upcoming resolution of the production issues with the games console – then you would undercut yourself and run your business into the ground. In this instance, complete honesty is trumped by necessary shrewdness.

The key takeaway from all this is that money in itself is neither good nor evil and should neither be avoided nor courted for its own sake. Instead, the wise person remains indifferent to its presence or absence – much as we should regarding health or fame. It might be a *preferred* indifferent – that is, something that might make being virtuous and happy easier – but it is not ultimately something that we should make a central goal of life.

I am aware that I've dwelt here on the view that money and possessions don't guarantee happiness (and can lead to its opposite), but obviously the main issue for most isn't the sudden loss of wealth, or its corrupting influence, but the hardship and suffering that *lack* of money brings. Stoic acceptance and indifference can help us deal with some of the consequences of poverty, and we will look more specifically at pain, illness and other such things later on (see page 122), but the general lesson is that we are *more* than our material trappings – even if it might feel that their lack makes us *less*.

'Now death and life, glory and reproach, pain and pleasure, riches and poverty – all these happen equally to the good and the bad. But, as they are neither honourable nor shameful, they are therefore neither good nor evil.'

Marcus Aurelius, *Meditations*, II, 11

Here, Marcus Aurelius gives his own take on the doctrine of preferred indifferents. We would all obviously prefer to be alive, well thought of, living a pleasurable existence among material comforts. But such things have no *moral* value – their possession (or lack) does not make a person good or bad. Therefore, we should be indifferent to them, for they serve no true role in the central purpose of our lives: to live virtuously and happily in accordance with Nature.

'We are all chained to fortune: some men's chain is loose and made of gold, that of others is tight and of meaner metal: but what difference does this make? We are all included in the same captivity, and even those who have bound us are bound themselves... All life is slavery.'

Seneca, *On Peace of Mind*, X

It is a striking image: we are all slaves to Fate, so what does it matter if our chains are made of gold? Someone who holds high office is as much 'enslaved' to his duties as a literal slave. This talk of slavery, which was a fundamental feature of both Greek and Roman life, often occurs in Seneca. Unlike Epictetus, Seneca only experienced slavery from the owner's viewpoint, but he nonetheless recognizes the hardship and misfortune of those trapped in it, and uses the metaphor to illustrate the invisible chains that even 'free' people are bound by: their passions and desires, their onerous work duties and the burden of family obligations, and so on. To be truly free is not something that wealth can buy; it must be achieved by an attitude of mind that sees all material trappings as ultimately irrelevant.

THINK ABOUT...

Whether we earn it, inherit it, win it or acquire it by less reputable means, money is a necessity. Similarly, unless we take the veil or join a monastery, it is also extremely hard to live completely without possessions. And, as Shakespeare put it, even 'the basest beggars are in the poorest things superfluous' (*King Lear*). Why bother with clothes? Or washing? Or anything at all that differentiates us from the animals? But most would agree that it is necessary to have *something* to wear, *somewhere* to live. Certain things are a minimum for some sort of civilized life. Though he threw away his bowl, even Diogenes held on to his cloak – and his barrel ...

It is not what we have, but our attitude to that which counts. We must condition ourselves to recognize that money, and the things it buys, are not permanent parts of our life. When you look around you, how much of what you own is essential? How much could you happily do without, and what would you miss if it were suddenly gone? In her book *The Life-Changing Magic of Tidying Up*, Japanese author Marie Kondo asks that we apply a simple criterion (the 'KonMari' method) to each thing we own: is it either useful or does it 'spark joy'? If neither, then we should discard it.

This is probably a useful exercise for us all, especially book hoarders (yes, I'm looking at *you!* Ahem ...), but for a Stoic, this would be to focus on the wrong thing. The correct attitude to possessions lies not in paring them back to useful essentials, beautiful *objets d'art* or sentimental treasures, but in recognizing that *none of these things* are 'possessions' at all, strictly speaking. They are things of which you are only in temporary guardianship – and which might disappear any day. The KonMari method might help you enjoy those things you love more, but it won't help you deal with their loss.

So, what will? The only thing you really own is your mind and how you react to things; or rather, to speak more precisely, *how you react* to how you react, for our impulses and emotions are often the first on the scene, with reason and judgement lagging a few steps behind. We will come back to the role of emotions later (see page 138), but for now have a think about how you might feel if you lost a treasured object. Why do you feel the way you do? Let's say it is your late grandfather's watch, or your wedding ring, or your top-of-the-range Mercedes. What about that loss would upset you? The economic outlay of replacing it? The memories that it spurs? The sense of ownership, as if it is somehow vital to who you are?

All of these things, the Stoic would say, are based on delusion, of one sort or another. If the economic cost of replacing the Mercedes is crippling, then why have you chosen such an expensive car in the first place? There are cheaper ways of getting from A to B. So, is it about status? Ego? Regarding the watch, are your fond memories and feelings about your grandfather tied to a leather strap, a few cogs and springs? It can't bring your grandfather back, and you should let him go, too. And unless we are talking about the One Ring (in which case, the preciousss is mineses! I mean, er, Sauron's ...), I doubt there will be massive practical

'These reasonings have no logical connection: "I am richer than you, therefore I am your superior." "I am more eloquent than you, therefore I am your superior." The true logical connection is rather this: "I am richer than you, therefore my possessions must exceed yours." "I am more eloquent than you, therefore my style must surpass yours." But you, after all, consist neither in property nor in style.'

Epictetus, *Enchiridion*, XLIV

Epictetus's logic is so simple and obvious, here: money, fine clothes, an expensive education, even superior talent – none of these things make someone 'better' than you, because these are not measures of moral worth (which is the only measure we should be concerned about). And yet it is a trap that we fall into every day, leading to envy, low self-esteem and other undesirable feelings. But nor should you fall into the opposite trap – that being 'virtuous', 'humble' or studying philosophy makes you superior to those shallow people who value only wealth. For your achievements and interests are equally at the whim of Fate, and as certain one day to disappear. And in light of which fact, no one is superior.

consequences to its loss; a marriage that dissolves over the loss of a hunk of metal is not much of a marriage, after all.

Some of these lessons may sound harsh, but the Stoic would argue that they are harsh *truths*. It is often said in relation to wealth that 'you cannot take it with you' (when you die). But if the Stoics are right, then there is also a sense in which you never really had it in the first place, for it was only ever yours on loan.

GOING FURTHER...

1. Choose a valued possession and make a list of what you feel about it and why. Where does its value lie? Is it very expensive, unique, beautiful, meaningful or does it have sentimental value? Now, how might you console yourself if it were suddenly lost or stolen? Does it help to think of it as a preferred indifferent, something that contributes – but is not essential – to your happiness? Doing this exercise will help you gain a different perspective on what role the prized item plays in your life, which you can then apply to all your possessions. So, once you've finished, maybe choose another item and repeat the exercise.

2. How much wealth is enough? As an exercise, imagine that you won the lottery. How much money would you need to change your life for the better? One million? Ten? More? What tangible benefits would it bring? List a few, then ask yourself whether these things might be achieved without the money – and if so, how. You might also list ways in which the money might make you potentially unhappy – generating arguments with family and friends, perhaps. You may find that wealth is not the magical cure-all for life's ills that you think it is.

3. One of the benefits of wealth is that it allows us to help others. In 2009, the philosopher Peter Singer (1946–) published *The Life You Can Save*, which argued that people living in affluent Western countries have a moral duty to help those living in poverty around the world. He has since set up an organization by the same name that encourages *effective altruism*, an approach that seeks to identify the causes upon which charitable donation will have the most impact. You can check out his book here – **www.thelifeyoucansave.org/the-book** – where you can also download a free copy. Or, of course, you can simply follow your own instincts and give to whatever charitable cause you care strongly about.

WORK

WHY IT'S NOT WHAT YOU DO,
IT'S THE WAY THAT YOU DO IT

3

If you've ever had a nightmare boss, then spare a thought for Seneca.

We have already had a taste of the Emperor Nero's bad side – extravagant overspending, random late-night killing sprees – to which can be added a monstrous ego (the Colosseum was originally so called for its proximity to the Colossus of Nero, a thirty-metre bronze statue of the emperor that towered beside it) and – well, more murdering, including his stepbrother, his wife and even his own mother, but really anyone who looked at him a bit funny or didn't clap loud enough at his singing and acting performances. We don't really know how much of his popular reputation is true – did he really play the lyre while Rome burned, or in fact set the fires himself to clear space for the construction of his Golden House? – but enough is well-documented to make us appreciate with what a heavy heart Seneca must have dragged himself out of bed every morning, knowing the mountain he had to climb.

Seneca was a very ambitious man and from early in life had set his sights on high office. Having become a senator, he made the mistake of giving too eloquent a speech and narrowly escaped assassination by the jealous Emperor Caligula (who was fortunately persuaded that the philosopher's ill health meant that he had pretty much one foot in the grave anyway – Seneca seems to have suffered from tuberculosis from a fairly young age). He was eventually banished to the island of Corsica by Caligula's successor, Claudius (10 BC–AD 54), for an alleged adulterous affair with the emperor's niece. This would have represented quite a blow for Seneca's career prospects and he consoled himself and others with typical Stoic advice (the works from this period are known as his *Consolations*, which consisted in various essays and letters). One was addressed to his mother, comforting her on the loss she must feel at his exile, and others were to various acquaintances who had suffered the deaths of family members. In these, he reminds us that our fate is not our own and that all of our disappointments and sufferings are trivial in comparison to the size of the world (which will itself ultimately pass away).

But just when he had settled down to a life of quiet, contemplative exile, he was suddenly recalled to Rome. He had been hired by Nero's mother, Agrippina (AD 15–59),

> '1 am as joyous and cheerful as in my best days: indeed these days are my best, because my mind is relieved from all pressure of business and is at leisure to attend to its own affairs, and at one time amuses itself with lighter studies, at another eagerly presses its inquiries into its own nature and that of the universe.'

Seneca, *Of Consolation: To Helvia*, XX

What happens when our ambitions are dashed? As already noted, Seneca harboured great political ambitions, and so his exile would have been crushing to him, but here he is writing to his mother, consoling her on his banishment to Corsica, and reassuring her that he is happy. Not only is he free from the stress of his previous role, but is now free to concentrate on philosophy and the things that really matter. Our failed ambitions give as much room for learning and growth as our achievements – in fact, more so.

'Do you not see the smallest plants, the little sparrows, the ants, the spiders, the bees, all doing their part, and working for order in the Universe, as far as in them lies?'

Marcus Aurelius, *Meditations*, V, 1

We may still draw occasional parallels with nature – we are 'busy as bees' or 'industrious as ants' – but we don't generally think of our jobs as allowing us to work together with them 'for order in the Universe'. But Marcus's point is that this is how we should think of our work, for we are as much a part of the natural order as are the birds, ants, spiders and bees. This idea of the interconnectedness of all nature is one that has gained scientific respectability in modern times through Gaia theory, as originated by English environmentalist James Lovelock (1919–2022), where Earth may be thought of as a self-regulating organism, each part of which serves the whole. And of course, aside from humanity's broader role in the natural order, we must remember the important part each of us plays in the *social* order too, through our work and personal interactions. All of which may lead us to question ourselves: are we playing that part to the full? How does our activity contribute to wider society? Look for the positive impact that your work has on the lives it touches. These might seem small but taken together they can add up to a significant difference. Try to bear that in mind as you go about your job.

to tutor the young emperor-in-waiting; perhaps she had already recognized that the boy needed taking in hand. Then when Nero eventually came to power (aged just sixteen), Seneca rose with him, his ambitions realized at last as he became the boy-emperor's advisor through the early years of his rule – a period which most historians consider to have been relatively well governed. Seneca would go on to become a very influential and powerful figure in Roman politics – until, finally falling foul of Nero's paranoia, he was forced to commit suicide (an event which we will come back to in a later chapter, see page 212).

Seneca was hired by Nero's mother not to teach the boy ethics or philosophy, but law, politics and rhetoric, which she considered a more useful education for an emperor-in-training than filling his mind with such concerns as 'how to be good', 'what is truth', and other such unsettling and impractical ideas! Hamstrung in this way, Seneca nonetheless tried to sneak those lessons in. For example, his work *On Clemency* is a not-so-subtle hint as to how the good and just ruler should prefer the path of mercy to that of the bloody road of retribution, strewn with the corpses of his enemies, favoured by the power-crazed tyrant. This was at a time when the concept of mercy would have been quite a hard sell in the ruthless Roman political scene, where an eye for an eye (and maybe a head, too) was often thought better political sense – and where possible, to get your retaliation in first.

I'm betting that Nero didn't read it. At any rate, he was more concerned with singing and acting than being a good emperor.

What can we glean from this – slightly depressing – episode?

Well, first of all, that we should thank our lucky stars that we are not Seneca! But whatever our working situation, it's likely that we will experience at least some trials, tribulations and disappointments. So, what is the key to overcoming these? One common source of workplace discontent is a failure to properly value what you do. Unless you really are working for the modern-day equivalent of a Caligula or a Nero, then there are likely positive outcomes that your work serves that you may be overlooking. From bankers to bin men, florists to fast-food workers, most jobs will provide some chance to develop our character and to help others. And doesn't society need all those roles? (OK, maybe not bankers ...) And of course, work can be enjoyable. Even Karl Marx (1818–1883), who thought that all forms of capitalist employment involved a degree of exploitation, was keen to emphasize that we are by nature *productive* beings, and that it is fundamental to human experience to engage in such activity – whether paid or not. A life without work might be boringly empty! So, look for the aspects of your job that you enjoy for their own sake, the things that drew you to this type of work in the first place – I'm sure there are some, even if you've forgotten them at the current time.

The other common gripe is the feeling that your skills and talents are being wasted. You have dreams you want to achieve! Novels you want to write! Films you want to direct! Hilarious TikToks you want to create! You want to be an artist! A musician! (Hmm, I hesitate to say this, but you *are* starting to sound like a certain Roman emperor ...) If only you didn't have to work all the time, slaving away for The Man just to pay the bills. If only you'd come from a wealthier background, or had connections, like all those lucky people who have made it big.

If you really feel a calling in such a direction, then there is absolutely nothing to stop you. Stoicism does not say, 'Know your place and don't rock the boat'. But it also doesn't say, 'Waste half your life on a pipe dream that your friends should have had the courage to point out was a non-starter from the get-go'. So, first of all, weigh up how feasible such a course of action is and how hard up it might leave you if you were to abandon your regular source of income. In other words, use your *reason*.

When Cleanthes first came to Athens, he wanted to study philosophy under Zeno, but he was extremely poor, with no means to support himself. And so, while he studied philosophy by day, he worked at night in various forms of casual menial employment – carrying water, digging ground, crushing grain, anything that would allow him to pursue his real goals. And, as already noted, Marcus Aurelius wrote his *Meditations* while running an empire and personally directing a military campaign in Germany.

If you are determined and serious enough, you will find a grown-up, rational way of following your calling. For the rest of us, maybe work isn't the problem; maybe it's *us*.

"'I would conquer at the Olympic Games." But consider what precedes and what follows, and then, if it be for your advantage, engage in the affair. You must conform to rules, submit to a diet, refrain from dainties; exercise your body, whether you choose to or not, at a stated hour, in heat and cold; you must drink no cold water, and sometimes no wine – in a word, you must give yourself up to your trainer as to a physician. Then, in the combat, you may be thrown into a ditch, dislocate your arm, turn your ankle, swallow an abundance of dust, receive stripes [for not training], and, after all, lose the victory. When you have reckoned up all this, if your inclination still holds, set about the combat. Otherwise, take

notice, you will behave like children who sometimes play wrestlers, sometimes gladiators, sometimes blow a trumpet, and sometimes act a tragedy, when they happen to have seen and admired these shows.'

Epictetus, *Enchiridion*, XXIX

This is excellent practical advice. Whatever dream you have that would replace your current work (for example, winning gold at the Olympics), think about what it involves. The incredible physical preparation and discipline that must come first, and the subsequent potential disappointment – or, perhaps, dealing with fame and public expectation. Think it all through. Is your dream still appealing? Epictetus points out that we are often like children who come away from some public entertainment wanting to be wrestlers or gladiators or musicians or actors. We must be on guard against such fickleness and lack of seriousness, and know it for the distraction and fantasy that it often is.

THINK ABOUT...

In a Gallup poll in 2023, it was revealed that, as a global average, a staggering sixty-seven per cent of people felt disengaged at work. This was a drop from eighty-five per cent in 2017, but still, not exactly encouraging. A further fifty-one per cent of employed people stated that they are actively seeking other work. Such numbers are quite astounding. Everyone has days when the stress or tedium of employment becomes too much for them – but for *most* of us to feel like that, *most* of the time? Do you? If so, apart from staring out the window while you dream of winning the lottery, or exacting subtle revenge through leisurely toilet breaks, surreptitious Facebook scrolling and other forms of 'quiet quitting', what can you actually do about it?

First of all, it will help us to understand what the precise issue is. If you dislike your job, why is that? Does it feel meaningless? Ethically compromising? Too stressful? Underpaid? Or just plain boring? All of these are good reasons to look for something else, but there is also the possibility that, underlying all such forms of discontent, you would simply rather be somewhere else – the beach, or the cinema, or just at home with your feet up. Maybe, then, it is work itself, and not any particular job, that is the issue. If so, the Stoics have a simple and clear answer for you: look at yourself, for both your discontent and your ability to change that reside in your mental attitude to your work – and that's really the only thing that's completely in your control.

'A man's master is he who is able to confer or remove whatever that man seeks or shuns. Whoever then would be free, let him wish nothing, let him decline nothing, which depends on others; else he must necessarily be a slave.'

Epictetus, *Enchiridion*, XIV

This gets to the root of our discontent with work: it is being controlled by another. No one knew this better than Epictetus, of course, and here he points out that total freedom can only be obtained by accepting that we have no power to wish for or avoid anything that depends on others. Even being your own boss is no solution, because that too will at some point involve things that you have no control over – which is pretty much everything outside of you. Complete autonomy exists only in the mind.

There will always be things that you don't want to do. This even includes things that you may have at some point voluntarily signed up for. Let's say that you land that dream job as ... I don't know, a croissant taster at the local pastry factory. You love croissants! But every day? After a few months, even the appeal of their hot flakey buttery goodness starts to pale; after a year or two, you never want to see another French pastry for as long as you live. Maybe if you worked hard, you could get that promotion to the cream cakes section – now there's a job you could never tire of ...

The point here is that, at some point in your working life, the grass is going to start to look greener somewhere else. One possible cause of this lies in that less-rational aspect of you which is fickle and short-termist, that seeks gratification now and wants perpetual distraction, novelty and fun. But, as Stoicism points out, it is not this part that defines you as a human being; it is the possession of *reason*. Yes, there are perhaps jobs that can satisfy this irrational part of you – that are higher earning, faster moving, less stressful, or whatever – for a while, anyway. But at some point, whatever you do, there will be days when you begin to feel just like Seneca – not trying to cram a crumb of decency into a spoilt amoral teenage tyrant who spends most of his time daydreaming of building giant bronze statues of himself and murdering his relatives, but simply overwhelmed at the prospect of yet another day filled with joyless, intimidating or dispiriting tasks.

So, what's the answer? Assuming that you're not some undiscovered genius smothering your creative ambitions beneath a dead-end job, then the answer likely lies in appreciating the positive value of what you do (for yourself and others) and understanding that – whatever your role – it is always *yourself* that you are working on. I'm going to bring in a word here that the Stoics were quite big on: duty – but not ultimately to your company, your profession, your parents and family, some Protestant work ethic, or even to society at large; to yourself. Your only duty as a human being is to be true to the rational part of you that weighs up your life goals and identifies those that best serve your personal growth. If that's a different job, fine; if it's a different attitude to the one you already have, then that's fine, too. Only your reason can decide that.

'The vain-glorious
man places his happiness
in the action of others.
The sensualist finds it
in his own sensations.
The wise man realizes
it in his own work.'

Marcus Aurelius, *Meditations*, VI, 51

'Work' here is being made to serve two senses. It is the everyday activity that we do to support ourselves and others, to earn money, to perform public services, and so on. But it is also work on oneself. For really – if everything that Marcus has said about the role that we play in the overall design is true – there is no difference between the two things. Whatever we do, we should employ the same principles – not for personal vanity and ego, and not for sensual pleasure, but to live virtuously in accordance with Nature – and thereby our actions will serve the common good.

GOING FURTHER...

1. Assuming that you are to at least some degree unhappy with your current work, take your present job and list the reasons for your discontent. Now go through each of them and try to identify what the reason for that is. Does the discontent lie in something you can change, or something you cannot? Your boss is a nightmare (let's say). You might complain about him to HR, have a clear-the-air conversation or look for ways to minimize your interactions. All these are good practical steps, but – the Stoic would point out – the only thing that is really under your control is your reaction to *him*. You cannot force him to change. So, while there is every reason to try to analyse that aspect of your work that is depressing you, the only thing you can definitely change is how you think about the situation. How might this approach help you?

2. Take Epictetus's exercise and apply it to some dream or ambition that you have. Have you really thought through 'what precedes' (the preparation, the hard work) and also 'what follows' (the potential disappointment, or even the downsides of success)? If you became a rock star or a sporting hero, what would that mean for your family life? Your friendships? Lastly, try to identify what fundamental drive you are serving in all of this. Is it ego? Fanciful whim?

Anticipated pleasure and wealth? Or something more meaningful? If your ambitions still seem realistic and justified, the sacrifice worth it, and will not lead you away from your greater duty to follow a moral path, then you have Epictetus's permission: go for it!

3. In terms of the big picture, consider in what way your current job affects society and the world as a whole. What is the ethical and environmental footprint of what you do? Many of us aren't lucky enough to work for organizations that are focused on making a direct positive difference to the planet and its creatures, but that doesn't mean that we can't make a difference in other ways. Are there initiatives that you could suggest that would improve your workplace's recycling practices, for instance, or ethical investments? Even small actions, undertaken by individuals, can have a significant accumulative effect.

HAPPINESS

WHY BEING HAPPY IS ABOUT
MORE THAN FEELING GOOD

CHAPTER

4

Are you happy?

Actually, don't answer that, because it's a bit of a trick question. For whatever you would have said (unless it was going to be, 'Well, what's happiness, anyway?'), my next question will be:

'How do you define happiness?'

Is it a feeling? A warm fuzziness inside that accompanies certain events or actions?

Or is it a set of achievements? The fulfilment of certain ambitions or goals?

Or is it perhaps a certain way of looking at things? A set of abilities, psychological attitudes or life skills? A glass-half-full sort of optimism?

Whichever of these responses you find yourself veering towards, you can see that each one emphasizes something different.

When we ask this question of philosophy, we get a similarly divided answer.

Utilitarianism (at least, in its original form) is mainly concerned with happiness in terms of how certain outcomes make us *feel*. Associated with such philosophers as Jeremy Bentham (1748–1832) and John Stuart Mill (1806–1873), it proposed that the right course of action is that which causes the greatest happiness (or minimizes the most pain) for the greatest number of people in a particular situation (and where 'happiness' is broadly defined in terms that relate to pleasure). This isn't to say that certain principles or rules aren't important – a utilitarian might still think killing or stealing is wrong, as a general guideline – but utilitarianism is flexible in a way that other moral theories aren't, and it all boils down to how a certain course of action will ultimately *make us feel*.

Another type of theory focuses on 'doing the right thing'. Such theories are called deontological or duty-based ethics and are associated with philosophers such as Immanuel Kant (1724–1804), who believed that what you feel and who you are is not as important as correct moral conduct. You might be a terrible person *inside*, seething with all sorts of resentments, amoral urges and general ill feeling, but as long as you can keep all that under control, do not steal, murder or lie, and respect everyone else's autonomy (treating them not as a means to your own ends, but as an end in themselves), then you can be considered a 'good' person. So, you have a rational *duty* to be good, which consists in following moral rules, simply because you recognize that it is the right thing to do.

Virtue ethics, on the other hand, *is* about your qualities as an individual. What you are inside matters as much, and sometimes more, than what you do. You care not for honour or fame, fine clothes or fine dining, focusing instead on developing the sort of personal traits and virtues that make you a decent person. This approach is associated with philosophers such as Aristotle and Plato.

Please excuse the crash course in Moral Philosophy 101 – I have simplified things a little here to give a general overview, the main purpose of which is to provide some context to the Stoics' approach to this question. Of course, while handy, we also shouldn't overemphasize the differences between these approaches: Bentham and Mill weren't just concerned with personal pleasure, Kant also wanted you to develop good character traits, and Aristotle thought that there were some general moral prohibitions (such as regarding murder) that we should abide by no matter what. Stoicism and Kant also agreed, against utilitarianism, that intentions were more important than outcomes, because you can control the former (giving someone good advice) and not always the latter (how that person receives and acts upon it). There is also a sense in which feeling, behaviour and character are all interlinked: what you do will determine how you feel, and who you are will determine how you act. But the real issue – when it comes to the question of what happiness is, or how we achieve it – is which of these approaches we use as a guide. Is it feeling, duty or character?

The Stoics' answer to this was that a happy person is someone who has developed certain virtues of character.

'All that you desire to compass by devious means is yours already, if you will but freely take it.'

Marcus Aurelius, *Meditations*, XII, 1

What a wonderful quote! Marcus's point here is that we are already befitted by Nature to be happy, and so in living in accordance with it, we will achieve those things we already desire. There is a type of satisfaction that comes from acting justly, from exercising rational control, from being moderate or courageous. By acting in these ways, accepting our lot and trusting in the natural course of things, we fill our true needs and are much happier than if we simply went after what we *think* we want.

This would seem to make Stoicism a type of virtue ethics and put it in the same camp as Aristotle and Plato – and it is true that they do share some common ground. Stoicism wanted to emphasize that a happy person is a virtuous person, and that acting virtuously – developing those traditional character traits (courage, wisdom, moderation, justice) – would most likely lead to a happy life.

In saying this, Stoicism directly opposed the *feelings* approach, best epitomized in their time by two philosophical schools: the Cyrenaics and the Epicureans. It is the latter of these that was the more influential and if we look at the dates of its founder, Epicurus (341–271 BC), we can see that he was pretty much an exact contemporary of Zeno, and it is Epicureanism that would eventually become the main opposition to Stoicism in the Greek and Roman philosophical world. An 'epicure' now indicates someone with a refined taste in food and drink, and such a person is most often now to be found eviscerating *Masterchef* contestants with supercilious putdowns of their failed beetroot and pomegranate soufflé. But the ancient Greek Epicurean was someone who actually professed moderation, favouring simple, mild pleasures over hedonistic excess or unruly ecstatic passions, and avoiding pain (as such, the philosophy may be seen as an early forerunner of utilitarianism). Like the Stoics, Epicurus thought the purpose of philosophy was to cultivate tranquility of mind (*ataraxia*), but whereas Stoicism saw pleasure as often disruptive to mental calm, and was therefore extremely distrustful of it, Epicurus argued that mental tranquility is a form of 'static' pleasure, such as the contentment we feel from a good meal or the gentle enjoyment of the company of a close friend.

This sounds quite appealing: a life spent pottering in the garden, taking tea with friends, a little reading, maybe, then a gentle stroll somewhere quiet – around the Garden, perhaps (the actual name of the place where Epicurus taught). To say, then, that the Stoics opposed this in favour of virtue brings to mind those po-faced Victorian parsons who inhabit BBC historical dramas or Jane Austen novels and are forever berating people for not attending church (the clue to which is 'berating', I think). But that's not really the sort of vibe the Stoics were going for. So, what did they mean?

It should be pointed out here that, when talking about 'happiness', we have been talking about the Greek word *eudaimonia*. But this is actually a word with quite different associations to its modern equivalent, and some translators will instead prefer 'flourishing', 'the good life', 'welfare' or some other term that suggests something deeper, broader and more meaningful than smiley face emojis or a five-year-old on a sugar rush. It literally translates as 'good spirit', *daimon* being linked to our modern word 'demon' but which for the Greeks meant simply a guardian spirit. Socrates claimed that he was guided by such a being and that it sometimes told him what to do and say. We can, therefore, think of *eudaimonia* as containing an element of 'taking the right path in life'. All of which makes 'happiness' seem a bit inadequate.

In disagreeing about the nature of *eudaimonia*, the Stoics and Epicureans were disagreeing not just about what would make you happy, but also were debating the true purpose of life.

'The best revenge is not to copy him that wronged you.'

Marcus Aurelius, *Meditations*, VI, 6

In the history of moral philosophy, the principle of 'do as you would be done by' has become known as the Golden Rule, which can be found in a diverse range of philosophies and religions. In the above quote, however, Marcus makes the same point not in terms of a principle of action, but in terms of character: don't *become like* the person whose actions have hurt you. For in seeking retribution – to take 'an eye for an eye' – we thereby indulge the very vices that led the other person to wrong you in the first place. Therefore, true 'revenge' lies in sticking to your own code of behaviour – which is, of course, not strictly revenge at all. What serves us best, best serves the other person too, for they may learn from our example.

For the Stoics, this involved being virtuous – brave, moderate, just and wise – because while there were times when doing good might bring pleasure, there were also times when it might not. A judge doesn't (or shouldn't) get a nice feeling from sending someone to prison, and it is rarely pleasant to tell someone a hard truth that they don't want to hear. But if we define virtue in terms of 'pleasure', then won't there be situations (dispensing justice, telling a hard truth) where we fail to do what's right because we don't like how that would make us feel?

But there is a further element that distinguishes Stoicism from Epicureanism and other philosophies, and that is 'living in accordance with Nature'. The happy Stoic was not only just and wise, but understood their place in the world and wisely accepted whatever (mis)fortunes Nature sent their way. In contrast, while Epicurus recognized that satisfying our basic natural needs was a prerequisite of happiness, he saw the natural world itself as the product of chaos, the random interaction of atoms (though interestingly, this did not make him an atheist). We will return to this question in later chapters, when we'll be taking a deeper look at who 'you' are and what exactly Nature is, as well as how to deal with unruly emotions. But for now, the main lesson to remember is that, for Stoicism, happiness is not primarily about feelings or performing certain strict moral duties, but in developing a good, virtuous character – from which the rest will follow.

> **'How many are the pleasures that have been enjoyed by robbers, rakes, parricides, and tyrants!'**
>
> Marcus Aurelius, *Meditations*, VI, 34

Not, of course, an advert for theft, debauchery, murder or tyranny, but an observation: if such terrible people have achieved so much pleasure, then how can moral goodness coincide with the unbridled pursuit of it? Like wealth and money, the Stoics saw pleasure as an 'indifferent', something that is morally neutral. But whereas we might naturally *prefer* to be healthy or rich, we should be much more on our guard with pleasure, because it often leads to vice. Obviously, as I've said, to completely deny ourselves pleasure is impossible, and there was some disagreement among the Stoics as to the correct attitude to adopt (some even thought it should be a *dispreferred* indifferent), but their general consensus was that pleasure should not be a guide to action. While it is not in itself immoral, pleasure *for its own sake*, without any moral code to curb it, becomes an irrational passion, and its overall effect on our moral conduct and mental equilibrium is a negative one. Pleasure, then – despite what Epicurus taught – cannot be the chief good. (A little unfair on Epicurus, perhaps, because we quite like gentle walks in the garden, but the general point is a fair one.)

'Pleasure-lovers spend every night amid false-glittering joys, and just as if it were their last. But the joy which comes to the gods, and to those who imitate the gods, is not broken off, nor does it cease; but it would surely cease were it borrowed from without. Just because it is not in the power of another to bestow, neither is it subject to another's whims. That which Fortune has not given, she cannot take away.'

Seneca, *Moral Letters to Lucilius*, LIX, 'On Pleasure and Joy', 18

This comes at the end of a letter to Lucilius, a Roman official serving in Sicily and one of Seneca's longtime correspondents. Lucilius's last letter had contained good news, which Seneca says it gave him great pleasure to hear – while admitting that 'we Stoics hold that pleasure is a vice'. There then follows a meditation on the sort of sensual pleasures enjoyed by drunkards, womanizers, the greedy and the ambitious, which may be contrasted with that experienced by those who strive for a virtuous life, and which may be more strictly called 'joy'. For unlike pleasure, this joy is not tied to any material circumstance, but is rather a by-product of being just, brave, moderate and wise. And not being gifted by (or subject to) Fortune, it is not something she can take away.

THINK ABOUT...

As I have said, for the Stoics the term 'happiness' is a much broader one than is now common. We are happy because we are virtuous, not because we cultivate a certain feeling inside. To go chasing feelings is a mistake, as is to stick to a strict set of rules or actions. Instead, we should try to embody the virtues in our daily lives. We should try to treat others fairly and live within established legal codes (justice). We should not let fear affect our choices (courage). We should cultivate moderation in relation to our desires and appetites, and check those tendencies in ourselves that disrupt our mental equilibrium or cause us to make bad choices (self-control or moderation). And we should try to base all our actions on self-knowledge, considered experience and calmly arrived at rational decisions (wisdom). All of these virtues are interrelated.

Picture a bad day. Your alarm doesn't go off, making you late for work. In your rush to the train station, you step into a deep puddle, soaking your leg up to the knee. Squelching into the office, somebody makes a quip at your sorry state and you snap at them, causing a bad atmosphere in the workplace for the rest of the day. Come lunchtime, you realize that you have forgotten to pack your sandwiches, and not having time to buy any, you have to make do with half a chocolate bar you find at the back of your desk drawer. Your hunger makes you even grumpier, and when you get home you quarrel with your partner over who forgot to put out the bins.

Now, let's rewind this. The alarm doesn't go off, but you set your annoyance aside – perhaps you forgot to set it, or perhaps it was a glitch – it doesn't matter. Shit happens. You are late for work, but more haste makes less speed, so you remember your packed lunch and are mindful of the puddle by the train station, because you are not chuntering away to yourself, still silently haranguing the ghost of Steve Jobs for the failure of your iPhone alarm. As a result, you're not hangry when you get back home from work, and so you don't snap when you and your partner realize that one of you has forgotten to put out the bins – perhaps it was you, perhaps it was them. So, instead of jumping down their throat, you make them a cup of tea. They've had a long day too.

The key to dealing with all these misfortunes (and yes, I know they're trivial) is not to sing a little happy song to yourself or chant a mantra; it is the courage to own your own mistakes, the mental clarity to treat others fairly, the self-discipline not to give in to your petty emotions, and the wisdom that tells you that 'stuff happens', 'we all make mistakes', 'things can't always go right', or whatever insight helps remind you that *you are not in control of everything that happens*. The corollary of which is, *nor is anyone else.* So, we should all cut each other some slack.

If we do this on a daily basis, choosing those actions and attitudes that help us stay on an even keel, then things get better. It's not an instant happy pill, but from this self-discipline and moral cultivation, we start to acquire a different sort of feeling; a calmness, a gentle acceptance. It's not always easy, and it's not always pleasant, but overall, over time, it does begin to draw us closer to being more responsible, rational, humble people, and closer perhaps to something we might broadly term 'happiness'.

'If you are dazzled by the semblance of any promised pleasure, guard yourself against being bewildered by it; but let the affair wait your leisure, and procure yourself some delay. Then bring to your mind both points of time – that in which you shall enjoy the pleasure, and that in which you will repent and reproach yourself, after you have enjoyed it – and set before you, in opposition to these, how you will rejoice and applaud yourself if you abstain.'

Epictetus, *Enchiridion*, XXXIV

Having said that Stoicism generally rejects *feeling* as a guide, here is an example where it is used to bolster virtue. But – and here is the key difference – the feeling is *secondary* to thought. You are tempted by some pleasurable experience which you suspect may not be good for you. The point, as always with the Stoics, is not to deny yourself pleasure (which is impossible), but to regulate it so that it doesn't overwhelm you. The goal is rational control and peace of mind, and we should only deny ourselves those things that threaten to develop into addictions, unruly passions, or simply are later regretted. As ever, Epictetus's advice is practical: if you think some temptation may be bad for you, don't rush into a decision, but try to find a moment when you are calm and consider how you will feel enjoying it, and weigh that up against how you will feel from having resisted. So, whether it concerns a cream cake or an extramarital affair, put yourself imaginatively in the situation and ask yourself which outcome you would rather. Often, you will make the right choice.

GOING FURTHER...

1. I mentioned earlier that there are competing views of happiness (see page 69). Which do you instinctively hold? Do you think of it as a feeling or mental state, a set of desirable circumstances, or a set of life skills? Make a list of what would be the case if you were 'happy'. What would change from things as they are now? If you find yourself wishing for external changes, remember that Stoicism argues that all such things are out of our control. Instead, then, try to think how you might rephrase your wish list in ways you *can* control. So, instead of wishing to have a less stressful job, wish instead for the mental calm to deal with stress at work. How might you achieve that? To start with, try to let go of those things you can't control.

2. Take some addiction, temptation or bad habit, and subject it to Epictetus's exercise. Imagine yourself first of all in full enjoyment of your pleasure – is it everything you think it will be? Next, think through the consequences, how it feels immediately afterward, especially any negative feelings. The point is not to guilt trip yourself into doing the right thing, but to make pleasure a process governed by reason. Cream cakes are lovely, but we all know that gluttony can lead to obesity, health issues and even have social side effects. Often, the key is not complete self-denial but moderation.

3. Consider Seneca's distinction between 'pleasure' and 'joy'. The 'higher' pleasures of being just, wise, moderate and courageous might seem too abstract and unachievable, but perhaps at first try to identify those pleasures that are less subject to fortune. Your favourite football team winning an away game might give you great pleasure, but their defeat at home send you into a spiral of despair. Is there perhaps a sweet spot where you can just enjoy 'the beautiful game', ignoring the ups and downs of victory and defeat, and – in the Stoic words of Rudyard Kipling's poem 'If' – 'treat those two imposters just the same'? Also try to identify the worst culprits, in terms of those things that cause the greatest emotional upheaval, and consider whether you might replace them with other pastimes. Thinking instead of drinking? Marching bands instead of one-night stands? (I don't know – I'm winging it here. I will leave you to find other rhyming substitutes.)

BELIEFS

WHY YOU'RE NOTHING TO THE
UNIVERSE, AND WHY THAT'S OK

5

What are you?

To say 'a human being' or 'a person' doesn't really tell us much, for what is that?

Modern science would say that we are bipedal, hairless primates (some of us more than others), evolved from the great apes, and socially orientated; that we are very intelligent, possessing dexterity and skill, the capacity for sophisticated forms of language and a high level of cognitive reasoning. Most religions – while possibly disagreeing with certain aspects of this picture – would add that, unlike animals, we possess a soul that lives on after death and that we are linked to God in some inextricable way, who, as our creator, may pass post-mortem judgement upon us, dispensing condemnation or blessing as He sees fit.

Intriguingly, the Stoic view differed from both these perspectives in certain ways, while concurring in others.

For instance, they agreed with Democritus (*c*.460–*c*.370 BC) and Epicurus (early pioneers of the atomic theory) that our soul, or *psychē*, is material, a mixture of the elements of air and fire. Therefore, if there is an afterlife, then it is likely that it would not be eternal, as the *psychē* would eventually disperse back into the elements from which it was composed. The souls of the virtuous and wise, being better regulated and organized than those of the unwise and unvirtuous majority, might persist in this post-mortem state for a bit longer, but even the most enlightened would eventually succumb to the 'Great Conflagration' that marked the end of world, wherein everything returned to the element of fire from which it originated – and from which a new world might then arise, as the cycle of creation and destruction began anew (and possibly, that history would repeat itself exactly as before). They may have been influenced in this view by the earlier Greek philosopher Heraclitus (*c*.540–*c*.480 BC), for whom the whole world was essentially composed of fire, which meant that everything was in a constant state of flux or change.

We may contrast the Stoic view with that of Plato, who saw the soul as *immaterial*, alleging that it survived the death of the body to be reincarnated in another physical form. But for the Stoics, only material things existed, and so the various thoughts, feelings, virtues and vices that make up a person are merely physical states or temporary patterns within the material *psychē* itself. (It is interesting to note here that a similar view persists in the modern Patternist or Functionalist philosophy of mind, where

'Why, then, seeing that the universe gives birth to beings that are animate and wise, should it not be considered animate and wise itself?'

Zeno of Citium, quoted in Cicero,
On the Nature of the Gods, II, 8

As already noted, the Stoic's God is not the Christian's (see page 20). Zeno and his followers adhered to a form of pantheism, whereby Nature and God were seen as the same being; or to put it another way, Nature is God's body, and God is the mind and soul of Nature. We are all a part of God/Nature, and the fact that we feel and think is evidence that Nature does too. For if a tree grew flutes or harps, Zeno points out, would we not assume that it had some inherent musical ability? He is, therefore, providing a sort of *cosmological argument*, arguing from a fact about the world (humans are conscious, intelligent, feeling) back to its cause (our creator – God or Nature – is too). In asking us to live in accordance with Nature, Stoicism is effectively advising us to align our attitudes and actions with those of the greater being of which we are a part – in whatever way we conceive of that.

a person's mind consists of the organization of neurons and synapses in the brain, as opposed to varying configurations of air or fire, and may therefore be capable of being preserved in the form of information – such as in a computer program.)

But the Stoics also shared with Aristotle the view that we are creatures whose nature is defined by the possession of reason, and argued that this rational faculty must play a central role in human life. Because of this, a virtuous person *must* possess wisdom or true knowledge, for without it, how can the other virtues of courage, moderation and justice be properly applied and ordered? How can we know which preferred indifferent it is appropriate to pursue, and when? God does not furnish our mind with knowledge from birth (as Plato thought), but it is more like a blank canvas, waiting to be written upon by experience, and out of which we must build up a picture of how the world is.

So far, so scientific(ish).

However, as we have seen, the Stoics considered the universe, Nature or God (which were all to them pretty much the same thing) to be a rational being, and argued that the key to acquiring the true knowledge on which to base a virtuous life was to align our own reason with that of the creator. For the Stoic, 'being rational' therefore took on a slightly different meaning to what it does today, for the reason in question was linked to the way the world is, where everything exists in a network of cause-and-effect which had itself been determined by God (the *Logos*).

If God is rational, then there is a reason for everything that happens. We may not always understand why this or that event occurs, but we can trust that it is right that it should, because it has been pre-ordained by a divine mind. This predestination also means that we have no say in what happens in life. A strict materialist would also point out that this should include thoughts and feelings, too, which are merely physical states of the brain and nervous system (and which therefore leaves no room for free will at all). However, the Stoic would resist this view (rightly or not) and argue that, if not free will in the fullest sense, we at least retain the mental freedom to choose how we *respond* to those events God pre-ordains.

Chrysippus appreciated this problem and his solution attempted to distinguish between 'necessity' and 'fate'. It's *necessary* I will die one day, because all physical events are *necessarily* linked by the laws of cause-and-effect; but *how* I die is not fated (how the story unfolds hasn't yet been written). So, I have a 'choice': like the dog tied to a moving cart, I can 'choose' to trot along happily, or pull back and resist, but either way I must move forward. Therefore, in a limited sense, I do have 'choice' (to walk or resist), and so free will is compatible with the necessary laws of physics (a view which has therefore become known as Compatibilism). However, this may seem like a cake-and-eat-it solution, and perhaps it doesn't work for you.

As you can see from the above, having said that the Stoics are materialistic and rationalist (a thing that aligns them with science), what we end up with is a very mixed bag,

'Everything proceeds from the universal intelligence, either directly or as a consequence. Thus, the jaws of lions, poisons, all evil things such as thorns or mire, are the consequences of the grand and the beautiful. Do not, then, imagine that they are foreign to that which you revere, but consider well the source of all things.'

Marcus Aurelius, *Meditations*, VI, 36

We can see here, perhaps, the beginnings of a response to the problem of evil, which Stoicism seems vulnerable to – at least, that which is called 'natural evil'. The danger posed by wild beasts, poisonous plants, and so on, as much as hurricanes and earthquakes, are mere by-products of an overall benignly ordered system. To illustrate Marcus's point, think of electricity, or cars, or any modern benefit to human life that has some dangerous aspect. Cookers, irons and kettles are not evil, but we nonetheless caution our children against getting too near them. Could we not think of natural evils in the same way? This, of course, is not an answer that will satisfy everyone, but it is an interesting angle. It may also be what the English poet William Blake (1757–1827) was getting at when he wrote in 'The Tyger', 'Did he who made the Lamb make thee?' Our concept of God, or Nature as a whole, is distorted by our human-centred perspective; but that does not mean that the whole is not 'good'.

which is in other respects closer to religion. The idea that God has created a world in which everything happens for the best will be difficult to stomach for atheists and those who reject traditional monotheism. How can the death of innocent children in natural disasters, war and acts of moral evil be considered 'the best' turn of events? The debate surrounding such questions – what is commonly known as the 'problem of evil' – has a long history in philosophy and theology, and I won't rehearse the traditional answers here, but let's just say that the controversy is ongoing, and there are no unproblematic answers.

So, where does all of this leave you? I don't want to presume as to what views you currently hold as to the nature of life, the universe and everything, and nor do I want to prescribe what those should be. I also don't want to squeeze or reshape Stoicism into a form that might be more compatible to the modern mind. But as you can see, there are different aspects of Stoicism that will appeal to different viewpoints, and it is really up to you as to which you find most palatable.

However, I think there are ways that Stoicism can be made to work, regardless of your metaphysical commitments. We may all agree that a great majority of the events that happen in our lives are out of our control. If the Stoics are right, then few things are *in* our control. If a freak wind causes you to fall out of a tree and break your leg, it is, therefore, immaterial whether these events are caused by God, Nature or the laws of physics, for the bottom line is, 'What do I do about my broken leg?'

The Stoic's answer is simply that we *accept* (well, after calling an ambulance). We train our minds to remain unperturbed by outer misfortunes and try to eradicate inner turmoil. *This* is what the Stoics meant by living in accordance with Nature. (What *were* you doing up that tree, by the way?) So, should we ignore the problem of evil?

Plato placed the centre of the *psychē* in the head, but Zeno situated it in the heart and lungs. Perhaps I'm being fanciful here, but this tells me that, instead of focusing on intellectual matters and getting lost in metaphysical controversies about the true nature of the world, the wise person concentrates on the experience of living – the beat of the heart, the motion of the breath. It is this living experience, and our conscious awareness of it, that most matters, whatever turns out to be the case regarding more speculative concerns. We can be wrong about the other things, but we cannot be wrong about that.

'We are all cooperating in one great work, some with knowledge and understanding, others ignorantly and without design. It is in this sense, I think, that Heraclitus says that men are working even while they sleep, working together in all that is being done in the Universe. Each works in a different way; and even those contribute abundantly who murmur and try to oppose and to frustrate the course of nature.'

Marcus Aurelius, *Meditations*, VI, 42

This expands upon the previous quote, but it goes further, for it introduces the idea that while some of us may work deliberately for good ends, even those agents that consciously *oppose* them are roped in without their consent or intention. To quote Seneca (who in turn is quoting Cleanthes): 'the willing soul, Fate leads, but the unwilling drags along' (*Moral Letters to Lucilius*, CVII, 'Obedience to the Universal Will', 11). This answers the other aspect of the problem of evil, namely, that of *moral evil*. The problem of natural evil asks how Nature can be good when there are scorpions, earthquakes and disease, whereas the existence of moral evil questions why God allows people to harm others and to work against His ends. Here at least we have a possible answer to the latter, for whatever immoral people do is made use of in the service of the overall benign design. Even evil serves a purpose.

'The duration of man's life is but an instant; his substance is fleeting, his senses dull; the structure of his body corruptible; the soul but a vortex. We cannot reckon with fortune, or lay our account with fame. In fine, the life of the body is but a river, and the life of the soul a misty dream. Existence is a warfare, and a journey in a strange land; and the end of fame is to be forgotten. What then avails to guide us? One thing, and one alone – Philosophy.'

Marcus Aurelius, *Meditations*, II, 17

This wonderful quote sums up the Stoic position: life is short, everything passes, all we have is our mind. Or, as Marcus Aurelius puts it elsewhere, 'We have body, soul, and intelligence. To the body belong the senses, to the soul the passions, to the intelligence principles.' (*Meditations*, III, 16). Of these, only the intelligence – what he calls the 'ruling part' or reason (what Stoics termed the *hêgemonikon*) – through the practice of philosophy, can be trusted to guide us through the false consolations of fame, power and wealth, the sensory illusions of earthly existence, and console us for the loss, grief and misfortune that Fate visits upon us. Sometimes, Marcus also talks of the mind as 'the immortal part', but this does not necessarily imply personal immortality, but merely the persistence of that quality that we share with the 'soul' of Nature. Besides, we shouldn't let such metaphysical questions sidetrack us into wasting our time, for, as he later points out (*Meditations*, III, 1), with ageing comes the possible loss and degeneration of our faculties, and with it the ability of the reason to rule. The time for happiness, virtue and inner freedom – to do the 'work', as the Stoics refer to it – is now.

THINK ABOUT...

What we believe, matters. Or at least, some of it does (we can set aside your opinion that The Beatles would have been an even better band if they had retained Pete Best as a drummer, or that tuna and banana pizzas are a crime against nature). This is because certain basic ideas can shape how we behave, our expectations, our attitudes. Inherited from environment, upbringing and our own life experiences, they often sit – for good or ill – unexamined and make themselves felt unconsciously, in such things as our general mood when we first wake up, whether we are more likely to consider ourselves lucky or to trust strangers. If you believe in some power that created the world for good, then it is more likely that you will have a positive view of other people and of life in general. The Stoics thought that God (or Nature) was a rational being with its own life and purpose, within which – to speak poetically – each human being was a single cell. You may or may not share that view, and I am not implying that only (pan)theists can be happy, but the point is that if we don't believe in *something*, then it is more likely that *nothing* will move in to take its place.

Nihilism is the belief that there is no God or benign power that created the universe and ordered it for the best, and therefore that life has no inherent meaning (which isn't to say we can't give it one of our own). In *Man's Search for Meaning*, the Austrian psychiatrist Viktor Frankl (1905–1997) recounts first-hand his experiences in the Nazi concentration camps during the Second World War. Observing those around him, Frankl realized that those who possessed some reason for living or had some unfulfilled purpose that they wished to live to complete – an unfinished novel or symphony, an unrealized personal or career ambition – were more likely to survive; whereas those who lacked such a thing were more likely to succumb to despair and die, regardless of their age or state of health. They succumbed to nihilism.

In his *Meditations*, Marcus Aurelius points out how insignificant we are in relation to the vastness of creation. What do our lives matter? What are our petty little plans and dreams in relation to the movement of the stars, the revolution of the galaxies, the enormity of interstellar nebulae (not that Marcus knew about galaxies and nebulae, but please allow me some poetic paraphrase here). But his point was not to depress you, or to argue that we should embrace nihilism; rather, he wanted us to take the pressure off ourselves. You think your problems are big? *This* is big. Otherwise, however, he maintained a positive belief in the meaningfulness of human existence, making an effort to be cheerful, to set achievable goals and to work on himself.

What do *you* believe? Are you a glass-half-full type of person? Or a 'grass is always greener on the other side'? The point is not to force yourself to adopt a sunnier disposition but to discover what your basic assumptions are – they may surprise you – and then to evaluate them. Do you have a firm basis for believing that, for example, people are generally selfish? Or that the toast always tends to land butter-side down? (Though really, you shouldn't be eating *anything* that has fallen on the floor, whatever side it lands on, in my humble opinion.) You may find that your beliefs don't have any such firm foundation. And whether you agree with the Stoics or not, it is in the *spirit* of Stoicism to subject your basic assumptions to rational analysis, to take ownership of what it is that you *do* believe – and where possible (if desired) to see if it can be changed.

'Suppose that [a man] has a retinue of comely slaves and a beautiful house, that his farm is large and large his income; none of these things is in the man himself; they are all on the outside. Praise the quality in him which cannot be given or snatched away, that which is the peculiar property of the man. Do you ask what this is? It is soul, and reason brought to perfection in the soul. For man is a reasoning animal.'

Seneca, *Moral Letters to Lucilius*, XLI,
'On the God within Us', 7–8

Here Seneca implicitly associates himself with Aristotle – that the defining characteristic of a human being is the possession of reason. External things – slaves, houses, income – are peripheral, subject to the whim of Fate, to which the soul or rational mind is impervious. Earlier on in the same letter, however, he comes curiously close to Christian doctrine: 'God is near you, he is with you, he is within you...a holy spirit indwells within us, one who marks our good and bad deeds, and is our guardian.' (1–2) We may of course translate all this into more naturalistic terms, but it underlines how Stoicism may take on a more or less religious tone depending on its practitioner (and, perhaps, the translator ...).

GOING FURTHER...

1. If you are keeping some sort of journal or have set aside some time for reflection (see page 30), consider in what way your reaction to any recent events may have been shaped by any underlying beliefs, especially negative ones ('This always happens to me', 'Why am I always ignored?', or whatever). The point is not to force yourself to 'look on the bright side', or remember that 'good things come to those who wait', because this makes the same (although opposite) mistake: assuming that you are *special*. In better understanding where our unconscious biases lie, we are in a better position to withhold our 'assent', as the Stoics term it – our instinctive inclination to consider something 'good' or 'bad'. Then the less likely we are to take whatever happens to us personally.

2. Book I of Marcus Aurelius's *Meditations* is a list of gratitudes – to parents, teachers, friends – thanking them for what they have taught him. Make your own similar list, trying to identify Stoic character traits or principles which you now believe yourself to possess because of other people. You can also include things that have happened to you, if you want, and what you have learnt from them.

3. Stoicism is not a set of rules to live by, but there are some simple tenets that it can be handy to bear in mind. Put these at the front of your journal, or pin them up, to remind you:

- Happiness is not a feeling or a set of circumstances; it is the result of living well.
- A happy life involves self-control, treating others fairly, acting courageously and acquiring self-knowledge.
- Accept that many things in life are out of your control; you can only change how you think about them.
- Death is inevitable and everything that you value is at the whim of Fate; prepare yourself for that.
- Treat misfortunes as tests or opportunities to build your character.
- The present is all you have. Do not worry about the future or regret the past.
- Try to remain calm and rational, and – where you can – distance yourself from disruptive people, situations and activities that create inner turmoil.

These are just some suggested core principles, but you can add to them as your understanding of Stoicism develops, rephrase them in your own words, or pick out your favourite quotes from the Stoics that embody them.

YOU

WHY WORKING ON YOURSELF
IS THE MOST IMPORTANT
THING YOU CAN DO

6

I think it is fair to say that we have become an age obsessed with identity.

By 'we' here I suppose I mean the technology-literate generation in Western countries (although by now it has become a global phenomenon) who began to hit their teens just as the Internet, smartphones and social media were really beginning to get going. So, those folk now commonly referred to as Generation Z or Zoomers, born somewhere between the mid to late 1990s and the early 2010s, and whom we might otherwise think of as 'digital natives', because they were the first to grow up with that technology already in place.

For this generation, and its children, self-identity has become an overriding concern. The need to define ourselves in terms of an increasing array of tribal characteristics that indicate anything from sexual preference, political ideology, sporting or musical affiliation, star sign, Myers–Briggs personality type, gender identity, even selecting or innovating bespoke pronouns. All this seems to stem from a sort of hyper self-awareness, and one of the key drivers in this is, arguably, the Internet itself. Online presence almost demands that we spend serious time creating a persona – a carefully crafted avatar, a witty or impressive potted bio – amassing an intimidating number of followers as we express our personalities through our comments, likes and shares, posed portraits of our lunch, our holiday destinations, our Pilates class, our pets – and of course, the ubiquitous selfie.

I am not necessarily denigrating any of this, by the way – most cultures have been 'self-ish' (to coin a term) in their own ways and to various extents, and the ancient Romans and Greeks were no different – and many of the above concerns can serve positive social functions. I am simply noting how intense all of this has become, and how different this 'obsession with self' is to what the Stoics thought of as 'working on your character'.

Identity and character are different things. That I am a fan of Taylor Swift may form part of my identity (I wear my hair like her, have TS-branded t-shirts, defend and promote her online, and so on), but I don't 'identify' as brave, or wise, or just – those are just characteristics that I have (or don't). Obviously, identity and character are interrelated – my Taylor Swift obsession (identity) may lead me to display my patience and determination (character traits) when virtually

'Are you distracted by the poor thing called fame? Think how swiftly all things are forgotten. Behold the chaos of eternity which besets us on either side. Think how empty is the noisy echo of acclamation; how fickle and how scant of judgement are they who would seem to praise us, and how narrow the bounds within which their praise is confined.'

Marcus Aurelius, *Meditations*, IV, 3

The lifespan of a Facebook post is a few hours; that of a tweet, something like fifteen minutes. But in comparison to the universe, our whole life is nothing but a TikTok – gone the moment it appears. How much less, then, is the value of those whose attentions you crave? Or their opinions? So, why chase fame? Why care what others think of you? By the way, we should note here that the 'you' referred to is not (perhaps) the reader, but Marcus himself, as the *Meditations* was really a private journal. Written in Greek (then the language of philosophy), its original title (although perhaps not Marcus's own) was *Ta eis Heauton*, which classicist Mary Beard translates as 'Jottings to Himself', and was never meant to be published. Which makes his observations all the more poignant.

'When things of great apparent worth present themselves, we should strip them naked, view their meanness, and cast aside the glowing description which makes them seem so glorious.'

Marcus Aurelius, *Meditations*, VI, 13

Whatever it is that we desire most – money, wealth, status, beauty – we can submit it to this test and see what is left. Your fancy wine is just grape juice, your fine clothes just animal hide or fleece, your expensive meal the dead carcass of a fish. The praise and adulation you crave is just wind from the flapping of lips, stained wood pulp or little flickering lights on a screen, all as ephemeral as the lives of the people who made them, and which themselves will also soon pass away. The only thing that matters – that endures – is being true to your self, the part of you that you share with the universal Mind, a thing that is completely *indifferent* to all these ephemeral trappings. (There's that word again!)

queueing for tickets for a concert. But mostly, 'I am going to work on my character' does *not* mean 'I am going to buy the new TS album and post rave reviews on all my socials'.

As previously noted, Stoicism is a form of virtue ethics, and shares with other philosophies (such as that of Plato and Aristotle) a belief in the importance of what are termed the *cardinal virtues*. As we have seen, these are wisdom, courage, justice and moderation. The philosophers who are considered virtue ethicists emphasized these character traits in different ways. For Plato, justice was not a separate virtue, but one that described the person who was in possession of courage, moderation and wisdom. A just person's character was therefore 'well ordered', in the same way that a just society displayed the right social qualities and institutions. For Aristotle, while the cardinal virtues were important, there were also other important virtues, such as modesty, generosity, public spiritedness and even wittiness, and that certain 'indifferents' (as the Stoics would later term them), such as health and a reasonable amount of money, were actually vital to living a fully ethical life. Furthermore, he argued that virtues (and vices) were something we acquired by practice – we aren't born wise or miserly or irascible – and a good guide to action is often the 'middle way'. Courage is a midpoint between cowardliness and foolhardiness, for example, and the correct balance is something we learn through trial and error, and the acquisition of practical wisdom (*phrónēsis*).

In slight contrast with the above positions, the Stoics considered there to be *only* four virtues, of which justice was a separate one (not a state springing from possession of the other three). They also agreed with Aristotle that virtue was something that we acquired by practice and through learning, for the good (or wise, or brave) course of action was not always an obvious one. However, because of their emphasis on the key role of reason, they argued that the most important virtue was wisdom, without which none of the other virtues could exist. To be brave, you must *know* what courage is and how to apply it; to be moderate, you must *understand* what that means in each situation, when to rein in this or that desire; to be just, you must not only have the strength to do the right thing when required – whatever the cost may be to yourself – but also *see* what that involves. In all these things, the intellect is key. A virtuous person is, above all, someone who is in firm touch with truth, and the Stoics believed, like Socrates, that virtue and vice are primarily matters of knowledge; we do not *knowingly* do wrong. And, as we've seen, most Stoics rejected Aristotle's idea that being virtuous required the possession of certain material qualities and goods – virtue was itself enough.

That said, with its emphasis on practicalities, the virtue that Stoicism most outwardly embodied was justice. The various anecdotes of the Stoics' lives that I share in this book illustrate how important actions are – often more so than words or ideas. So, while wisdom or knowledge are the sap of an ethical person (to use a botanical analogy), its flowering is justice.

The meaning of 'courage' is fairly self-evident, though obviously a brave person is not one who is always prepared to fight – in fact, there may be occasions where this is precisely the *wrong* thing to do. A person who speaks their mind before a dictatorial emperor may be considered just as courageous as the person who stalwartly faces imminent death (and given some of the personalities that occupied the imperial throne, this often amounted to the same thing). Courage can also be embodied through acceptance – of grief and loss, illness and disease, or of whatever Fate may throw at us.

Perhaps the trickier virtue to define, from a modern standpoint, is moderation. This is a translation of the Greek term *sophrosynē*, which has also sometimes been translated as 'temperance', 'self-control', 'decorum' or even 'soundness of mind'. It represents a sense of balance, of knowing when something is *enough*, *too much* or *too little*. It involves keeping the passions and desires in check – for food, sex and other pleasures – but not in such a way that eliminates them completely. Rather, Stoicism counselled *apatheia*, from which we get the modern word 'apathetic', but which for the Stoics meant a freedom from passion. But they were not trying to root out all feeling, merely trying to ensure that the irrational nature did not overwhelm the rational one – though they did not think 'reason' and 'desire' were separate parts of ourselves, but rather different aspects or ways in which the whole person could feel or act.

Returning to the Internet and modern life, how are we to apply this lesson? With the ever-increasing digitization of our day-to-day existence, complete withdrawal seems like less and less of an option. Besides, this would be to throw out the baby with the bathwater, for there are many benefits that the online world has brought us. The issue is, rather, how we can remain true to ourselves in a medium that favours shallow and fragmented interaction over genuine connection, that would rather generate the heated froth of controversy than meaningful debate. The answer, it seems to me, lies in the very virtues that the Stoics praised: the courage to speak our own minds and be true to what we believe, the wisdom to look for the truth with those who may not share our views, the temperance to rein in our own inflamed opinions and discontent, and the just desire to treat others fairly and – where necessary – to fight to change the system.

'If anyone tells you that a certain person speaks ill of you, do not make excuses about what is said of you, but answer: "He was ignorant of my other faults, else he would not have mentioned these alone."'

Epictetus, *Enchiridion*, XXXIII

I love the self-deprecating humour here: 'Why did he stop bad-mouthing me there? He obviously doesn't know me very well!' Self-knowledge is the key to happiness. If we are offended by what others think or say about us, then what exactly is being offended? Our ego? Our vanity? For either the critic is right – in which case we should thank them – or else they are wrong, in which case we should pity their ignorance.

'Remember that you are an actor in a drama of such sort as the Author chooses – if short, then in a short one; if long, then in a long one. If it be his pleasure that you should enact a poor man, or a cripple, or a ruler, or a private citizen, see that you

act it well. For this is your business – to act well the given part, but to choose it belongs to another.'

Epictetus, *Enchiridion*, XVII

There is a fore-echo here of Shakespeare's 'All the world's a stage' (*As You Like It*), proving that the analogy of life as a play, and people merely actors, is an ancient one. We have no say in the role we are allotted, so concentrate less on your costume and the number of your lines, or even the audience's applause, and more on how well you play your part.

THINK ABOUT...

It is common to conflate self with personality, but they are not necessarily the same thing. 'Personality' comes from the Latin *persona*, meaning a mask. It is the outward-looking face we present to the world. This may be contrasted with the inner or true self that only we can experience and know.

If you consider yourself to be the sum of your interests and passions, then the Stoics would argue that you are identifying with ephemeral and temporary things – with *externals* – and not with your true self. For how can you distance yourself from your emotions and desires if they are bound up with who you think you really are? If you think of yourself as essentially ambitious or funny, a party girl or a lone wolf, then what happens when those qualities become problematic or the source of pain? But what is this true self?

I have already briefly discussed Stoicism's metaphysical beliefs, and you may remember that their answer to this question is, 'We are rational souls'. But before you assume that they have in mind some incorporeal entity that floats around the ceiling at seances, let me go into a little more detail. To do this, I need to provide a bit of philosophical background.

There are two extremes in the philosophy of mind: dualism and materialism. Broadly speaking, dualists believe that a human being is made up of soul (or mind) and body, while materialists believe that we are just bodies and that the basis for our minds is therefore physical (the brain). So, for instance, dualists like the French philosopher René Descartes (1596–1650) argued that, since I can only be sure that 'I' exist, then I must be essentially a 'thinking thing', a non-physical entity different from my body. Similarly, Plato held that our soul is incorporeal and survives death in order to reincarnate in a different body.

Epicurus, on the other hand, was a materialist. He believed, as do most modern scientists, that we are just our physical bodies and that when we die our constituent atoms simply disperse. Materialists are therefore also *monists*: only one substance exists (physical bodies).

So, what about the Stoics? First of all, they shared Epicurus's belief that only matter exists (though not his atomism); however, they also shared with dualists the idea that the soul (which Stoics believed was basically a fine form of matter) could be separate from the body and could exist (for a while) after death. In this way, they could argue that you are *essentially* your soul or mind. Unlike Descartes and Plato, however, they did not deny that the soul contained 'irrational' aspects – our emotions and impulses are part of us, too. But it was our unique possession of reason that allowed us to control and limit these irrational aspects.

So, what does this mean for who you think you are? Well, for sceptics, it means that practising Stoicism does not require belief in some incorporeal essence. For those inclined to some sort of spiritual belief, on the other hand, it does not rule out hope of *some* sort of post-mortem existence (so perhaps you'll be floating round the seance rooms after all). I believe that's called 'win–win'.

In practical terms – and this is the key lesson that I draw from all of this speculation – it means that your unity and coherence as a person stems from *how much work you put in*. Through exercising our rational part (what they termed the *hêgemonikon*), we could acquire self-knowledge and practical wisdom, dampen our emotions and curtail our passions so as to achieve mental tranquility (*ataraxia*). In more prosaic, everyday terms, it means *not* losing your temper over some trivial tweet, *not* getting drunk and insulting your in-laws, and *not* trying to cheer yourself up by blowing your month's wages on retail therapy. Your bad habits and behaviours can be changed, because there is a sense in which *they are not you* – or at least, not what you *can* be.

'I have wondered often how it comes that, while every man loves himself beyond all others, yet he holds his own opinion of himself in less esteem than the opinion of others.'

Marcus Aurelius, *Meditations*, XII, 4

Marcus is also often fascinated by why we are so concerned with what others think of us. Why do we value others' opinions so much? It is as if we are building some fragile edifice that can be toppled by a cruel word. And that's really what most self-identities are. Why not, then, let the whole house of cards fall? All that really matters is acquiring a clear and accurate picture of ourselves. Others can help in that, but ultimately self-knowledge is a private matter. And if you don't trust yourself to make that judgement, then how can you trust yourself to believe what others say?

GOING FURTHER...

1. Produce a little potted biography of yourself, perhaps based on ones that you use for social media or some other online presence. List the things that you consider to be 'you' – things other people ought to know – such as your job, interests, nationality, sexuality, personality quirks, allegiances (political, sporting – whatever). Now go back through this list. How much of this is actually 'essential'? Which could feasibly change over time? And which, if any, are an expression of moral characteristics? The aim here isn't to produce the ideal Stoic pen portrait of yourself – I think that might be a contradiction in terms! Or at least, not something that you might want to use on social media. Rather it is just to get you to think about your conception of who 'you' are – and what you might become.

2. How much time do you spend online? There are various apps or in-built features for mobiles and computers that will tell you this, but if you don't have those, you can just estimate. Now, how much of that might a Stoic consider meaningful? There is staying in touch with friends and relatives, of course, keeping up with the news, involvement in social issues and causes. But how much is spent crafting a digital persona, or indulging in mental fantasy or titillating gossip? And how meaningful is that?

3. Take a sheet of paper, or open a document on your computer, and make a table with three columns and five rows, like so:

	✓	✗
Courage		
Justice		
Moderation		
Wisdom		

Now, next to each virtue, list a time when you displayed courage, and a time when you did not. Now do the same for the other three: a time when you did/didn't treat someone fairly, show self-control, and evidence self-knowledge or prudence. None of us is totally (im)perfect, so you should easily be able to fill all eight boxes. Now, consider your current situation and the things that are happening in your life. Are there opportunities to develop any of these characteristics? Toxic or abusive relationships that you can jettison or try to change? People with whom you could be more understanding or compassionate? If you find this exercise useful, consider doing it periodically.

HEALTH

WHY IT'S NOT ALL IN THE MIND –
BUT THE ANSWERS ARE

7

How are you?

It is a common enough question, which we ask – and are asked – almost every day. Though we rarely mean it. Not that we don't care about others, or they about us, but we all understand that such a question is not generally intended as a cue to share your every ache, pain and minor ailment. For we all have them, and the more of them the older we get. And if we suffer from a chronic illness, then we tend not to share that either – it's old news. Who wants to hear about that?

I am aware that not everyone is like this, or at least not all of the time, and that things may also differ according to place and culture and age, but I do think that generally, for most of us, our everyday health concerns are not something that we tend to broadcast. Unless there is a dramatic new medical development, such things tend just to tick over in the background, the private focus of perpetual low-level worry and monitoring. Should I see the doctor about that curious rash, that click in my knee, that annoyingly persistent cough? As I say, such things accumulate as you get older, but we try not to dwell on them or share them – for once you start, the list might never end ...

So, mostly we just answer 'fine', or 'Well, I've still got that thing with my back, but otherwise I'm OK', and the pleasantries exchanged, we move on to more interesting topics of conversation.

Are we being Stoical here? Sort of. If by that you mean, 'Health is only a preferred indifferent and we're all mortal anyway, so if you don't mind, I'm not going to talk about it.' But is that all Stoicism has to say about ill health, then? That we should just shut up and put up with it?

Well, no.

It is true that Stoicism will not provide you with detailed health tips – Gaius Musonius Rufus (first century AD) was a vegetarian, as was Seneca for a while, but there is no Stoically recommended diet, such as the Pythagorean injunction against eating beans (which stemmed, apparently, from their belief that the beans might contain departed souls – the same reason they were vegetarian). Cato the Younger (95–46 BC) was a soldier, Cleanthes was a boxer and Chrysippus was a long-distance runner, but there was also no recommended Stoic regimen of exercise or fitness programme.

Which is not to say that Stoicism cannot contribute to a healthier you, and there are, of course, indirect health benefits to adopting a Stoic way of life. For instance, practising the

'Men are disturbed not by things, but by the views which they take of things.'

Epictetus, *Enchiridion*, V

This statement is perhaps the cornerstone of Stoicism. Whatever happens to us in our lives, it is up to us as to how we take that. Even death, Epictetus says, need not be considered terrible, for it is a natural and inevitable thing. As for illness and other misfortunes, these too are natural events that come to us all at various points in life. When they do, the answer lies in not adopting the common negative view of such events, but in considering them calmly and rationally. So, 'Illness is not always avoidable, and something like this is bound to happen to me at some point'; 'It does not affect my ability to think and reason, and therefore does not disrupt my ability to be happy'; 'It may give me the opportunity to develop my strength and courage'; and so on.

'Sickness is an impediment to the body, but not to the will unless itself pleases. Lameness is an impediment to the leg, but not to the will; and say this to yourself with regard to everything that happens. For you will find it to be an impediment to something else, but not truly to yourself.'

Epictetus, *Enchiridion*, IX

Here Epictetus expands upon his earlier point (see page 125). Illness only affects our ability to be happy if we let it. A broken leg, a dicky heart, an irritable bowel – none of these things need affect the mind, specifically not the *will* (that is, our ability to assent to or deny that something is 'good' or 'bad'). As long as we retain the ability to choose how we view such ailments, then we retain the ability to be happy. Whatever our initial and natural reactions, then, we are fundamentally faced with a *choice*. Incidentally, Epictetus himself suffered his whole life from a crippled leg, either from birth or the result of an injury received in service to his master, so his advice here is grounded in personal experience.

virtue of moderation will make it less likely that you will overindulge in life's little pleasures, and therefore also be less prone to being overweight, or to suffer from the associated ill-effects of alcohol abuse or drug addiction – or sex addiction, for that matter (which, my Hollywood friends tell me, *is* a real thing, honestly). You will, therefore, be more likely to sidestep type 2 diabetes, cirrhosis of the liver, kidney disease, and other negative by-products of sensual overindulgence, not to mention awkward conversations with your GP.

There are also obvious health benefits to the Stoic way of dealing with emotion and the 'passions'. Even materialistic modern science is coming to accept that the mind and body mutually affect one other, so it only makes sense that the calmer you are mentally, the healthier you will be physically. As I've noted, the Stoics called this state of mental calm *ataraxia* (which roughly translates as 'impassiveness'), although like *eudaimonia* (happiness), it was a term common to a number of different philosophical schools, including Epicureanism. There are obvious Buddhist parallels here, such as with the concept of nirvana (which may be broadly rendered 'a windless state' where we are no longer 'blown about' by our desires), but we should also resist too close an identification of the two approaches. The Buddhist nirvana is a state of desirelessness accompanied by a loss of the usual sense of self (replaced, perhaps, by identification with the greater self or 'Buddha-nature' that pervades the universe), whereas the goal of Stoicism was not to eradicate all emotion or desire, and nor did they see the self as an illusion to be overcome. But there is undoubted common ground here, and the Buddhist idea that we can achieve this state of calm through relinquishing attachment (to things, people, ideas, feelings) is not so far from the Stoic's advice to focus only on those aspects of yourself (namely, your mind or soul) that are within your control and to let Fate have its way with the rest of you.

So, in summary, the Stoic attitude to health was a two-pronged approach. Through the practice of moderation and detachment, we might achieve both physical and mental health (*ataraxia*). And through a clear understanding of our true nature (that we are essentially rational souls or minds), we may more easily accept whatever bodily misfortunes, disease, pain and general suffering Fate may throw in our way.

This seems like good, practical advice. Who needs quacks and shrinks anyway?

But as with all things Stoic, there is a balance to be struck, which in health terms is somewhere between neurotic hypochondria, on the one hand, and the sort of alarming indifference to one's own bodily integrity ('Ah, it's only a scratch!') that should rightly remain the stuff of comedy sketches. Illness and disease are an unavoidable part and parcel of life. Some of this we can – and should – monitor carefully, and wisdom lies in knowing for which things we should enlist the help of professionals. Of course, you may live in a place or circumstances where access to such medical assistance is (for whatever reason) limited and unavailable. We should also remember that health is relative and science is progressive – we are mere generations in advance of those who died from diseases and conditions that we now

> '**Between the insanity of people in general and the insanity which is subject to medical treatment there is no difference, except that the latter is suffering from disease and the former from false opinions.**'

Seneca, *Moral Letters to Lucilius*, XCIV,
'On the Value of Advice', 17

There is a statement – sometimes attributed to Chrysippus, but common to many ancient writers – that 'everyone is mad'. Apart from, that is, the 'Stoic sages', who – because of their exemplary virtue and super-rationality – are the only ones not driven to 'crazy' behaviour by ignorance and irrational impulses. This is an example of a 'Stoic paradox', an apparently contradictory statement that was intended to challenge common assumptions. Others might be 'only virtue is good' (contradicting the idea that health, money and so on, are good too), or 'a wise man is free, even if a slave' (because only he is free from desire and delusion). Here Seneca acknowledges this truth, but also points out that genuine forms of mental illness require professional treatment. Those suffering from mental illness need a doctor; everyone else needs Stoic medicine.

'Men seek retirement in the country, on the sea-coast, in the mountains; and you too have frequent longings for such distractions. Yet surely this is great folly, since you may retire into yourself at any hour you please. Nowhere can a man find any retreat more quiet and more full of leisure than in his own soul.'

Marcus Aurelius, *Meditations*, IV, 3

Why go on holiday, when you can retreat into the calm of your own mind? Or, as Marcus more picturesquely calls it, 'the little field within' (IV, 3). The truth is, of course, that for many of us, our 'little field' is not a calm place to which we can retire, and we go on holiday to seek external distraction *from* our inner turmoil and tumult. But Marcus's point is that this shouldn't be the case. If we calm our emotions, desires and inner chatter, we not only circumvent the need to seek external sources of relaxation or refreshment, but we do so in a way that is not subject to travel delays, cancelled flights or flash flooding.

routinely cure, and future generations will no doubt look back on our benighted medical ignorance with pity and alarm. Stoicism is obviously of direct help here. 'Disease' is 'death' writ small. We are mortal and fragile, and we should not obsess about those things we cannot change.

The same goes for mental health. Stoicism does not imply that all mental illnesses are simply 'in the head' and we just need to man up and push on. This has been a prevalent attitude in certain places and times – and still is – and it is a harmful one. We all sometimes need help, whether personal or professional, and there is no shame in admitting that – in fact, it is *overcoming* the shame which is often half the battle. But where Stoicism can help is in alleviating those things we *can* change – that is, our attitudes to our illnesses. What we can change, we should; and what we can't, we should accept, whether mental or physical.

THINK ABOUT...

To the Stoics, as already noted, health was a preferred indifferent. Being healthy does not make a person more or less virtuous, and therefore we should not seek it for its own sake. That said, a life without health is much harder than a healthy one, and it also (some Stoics argued) affects our ability to live virtuously and be of benefit to others. And so, all other things being equal, we would much *prefer* to be healthy than not.

One of the main appeals of Stoicism is that it gives us tools for coping with such things as illness and suffering, whether mental or physical, and to whatever degree. And when you are ill, as much as you might *prefer* not to be, there may be nothing you can do about it. So, how can Stoicism help?

If you currently suffer ill health or chronic illness, then it can be hard to see your position clearly. Illness can lower our energy reserves and pain can cloud our judgement. But whatever the case, remember that it is only ever our *judgements* that are within our control anyway – nothing else. In light of which, Stoicism would recommend two things.

First of all, accept. Whatever treatments you are undergoing, and whatever the chances are of your recovery or improvement (and you should by no means give up on medical assistance), you are ultimately in the hands of Fate, however you define that. Therefore, accept that, and try not to focus on a particular outcome. To be 'happy' and to be 'well' are not the same thing; the former is within your power, whereas ultimately the latter is not. There is a calmness and freedom that comes from giving yourself up to whatever will be.

Secondly, put things in perspective. Illness, pain and disease are a natural part of life – as is death. All things that live will experience these things eventually, and so you are not alone. Don't allow morbid or self-pitying thoughts to overwhelm you, and resist the temptation to think of yourself as unfairly singled out by Fate. We are all at some point or in some way better off than someone somewhere else, and in letting go of bitterness we leave room to appreciate what life we have left.

If you are currently in good health – congratulations! – then you can, of course, set aside the above advice for a painy day (sorry …). However, you should also spare a thought for those in pain and suffering. Health might only be a preferred indifferent, but its absence can affect their mood and depress their outlook. And not all wounds are visible – yet one more reason to be charitable in our daily dealings with our fellow humans.

A final word about hope. When we are ill, the thought that pushes most of us on is the expectation that we will one day get better. 'I'm on day eight of the flu, so I should start feeling better in a day or two.' This is natural, of course, and whenever we hear of someone else's health troubles, we tend to try to help them 'look on the bright side', as if it is all just a matter of waiting it out. But sometimes, of course, time does not heal all wounds, and so counselling hope is misplaced. For this reason, Stoicism doesn't try. This may sound harsh, or even morbid, but – to repeat the mantra – none of this is within your control! So don't hope to feel better; feel better for giving up hope! There is no tomorrow that can make you well. Only today can do that. And that power is in your mind, your attitude and your thoughts – right now.

'I should prefer to be free from torture;
but if the time comes when it must be
endured, I shall desire that I may conduct
myself therein with bravery, honour,
and courage. Of course I prefer that war
should not occur; but if war does occur,
I shall desire that I may nobly endure
the wounds, the starvation, and all that
the exigency of war brings. Nor am I
so mad as to crave illness; but if I must
suffer illness, I shall desire that I may do
nothing which shows lack of restraint, and
nothing that is unmanly. The conclusion
is, not that hardships are desirable, but
that virtue is desirable, which enables
us patiently to endure hardships.'

Seneca, *Moral Letters to Lucilius*, LXVII,
'On Ill-Health and Endurance of Suffering', 4

The Stoic is not a masochist, seeking out hardships through a twisted sense of gratification. Rather, they seek to develop their character so that whatever hardships occur, then they will be prepared to endure them. Unlike torture and war, however, illness is much more likely, and so we should all adopt a mindset that would best help us deal with it. And what is that? Be brave, be calm and rational, seek solace in a philosophical understanding of *why* this is happening to you and why it need not be unendurable.

GOING FURTHER...

1. I was about to write 'Make a list...' when I realized that you may have had enough of them, so this time you are going to draw a picture. Something like this:

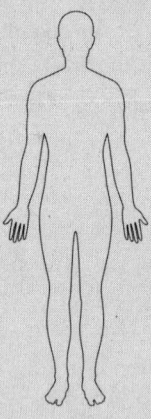

Now, label it with all your health issues and complaints – dodgy knee, carpal tunnel, depression – anything that you think affects you in any minor or major way. Once you have done that – oh, still going? OK, I'll wait a moment ... OK, once you have done that, think about what these things stop you from doing. If anything, what could you replace that activity with? If it causes ongoing pain or distress, is there anything else you could do to alleviate that? Other people whose advice you can ask? Once you have got these out of the way, after all the pills and treatments, all the physiotherapy and psychotherapy, you are left with the things you cannot change. This is where your Stoic training comes in. So, what should you do with these things? Accept them. Use them to develop your strength, your courage, your understanding of what this all means. Not easy things to do, I know, but the strength you develop in doing so will serve you well in all aspects of life.

2. Marcus Aurelius talks of retreating into 'the little field' – a state of mental calm (see page 130). As I have already said, for various reasons, most of us may find our minds more like a fly-tip than a rural oasis, and there may be some gardening and clearance work needed before we can feel refreshed there. One means of doing this is meditation. There are many forms of this, so have a look around and see what might work for you.

3. Go and visit a friend, relative or acquaintance and ask them how they are. Allow them the opportunity to open up about what's going on in their lives – if they want to – and encourage them to share. Then just sit and listen. Don't offer advice, necessarily, just allow them to unburden. Not only will this take your mind off your own concerns, but it will also help you see that there are more of us suffering silently than we might think.

FEELINGS

WHY YOU CAN'T CHANGE HOW
YOU FEEL, BUT YOU CAN CHANGE
HOW YOU THINK

8

The key to peace of mind is acceptance, and the key to that is to manage your feelings.

But what are 'feelings'? It can be a vague term. Your partner hurt your feelings when they implied that your new clothing purchase made you look fat. Obi-Wan had a bad feeling about his headstrong young apprentice. Feelings can include emotions, but it is a broader, more inclusive term, also involving things that are closer to sensations. Fear and excitement aren't quite emotions. Anger is a feeling, but annoyance is not quite an emotion.

All this may just be a matter of semantics, of quibbling over word definitions, but I think the broader definition is more useful here as we are going to talk about the wide range of things that can upset our rational control of ourselves.

The Stoics distinguished between general everyday *feelings*, which are natural and unavoidable, and *passions*, which are that subset of strong feelings that involve the overwhelm of reason by a powerful emotion or desire. It is such mental disturbance that leads us away from virtue and happiness, and into the realms of misjudgement and self-torment. But it is not wrong to feel fear, or sexual desire, or hunger – how could we not? Such things we share with the animals, and even in humans they form the natural basis for such positive things as love and affection, or parental protectiveness (as anyone will agree who has observed a female dog or cat nurturing its young). But strictly speaking, an animal does not experience passion, because it has no reason to be overwhelmed; nor, the Stoics would say, do children (which is perhaps one reason why the two are often lumped together in the famous piece of acting advice never to work with either). Adult humans, on the other hand, may control their natural impulses through rationally guided will. Whether you agree with these distinctions (and Darwin and various childhood psychologists might not), the point is that adult humans have a greater mental capacity to control themselves.

Stoicism identified four main types of passion that we should consider dangerous: fear, lust, mental pain and mental pleasure. Fear is an attempt to withdraw from some expected imminent threat or danger. Lust is a reaching out towards something that is desired but not yet obtained (which can include anger, if we consider that to be a lust

'When any person does ill by you, or speaks ill of you, remember that he acts or speaks from an impression that it is right for him to do so. Now it is not possible that he should follow what appears right to you, but only what appears so to himself. Therefore, if he judges from false appearances, he is the person hurt, since he, too, is the person deceived.'

Epictetus, *Enchiridion*, XLII

Epictetus here is attempting to switch around the way you see things. When someone offends or hurts you, the temptation is to pity yourself and to feel angry. Instead, he argues, we should pity the person who has hurt us, for their actions or words are based on an incorrect assumption about you. So, by relying on their own incorrect view of you, they have only hurt themselves. It is quite simple really: did you deserve their behaviour towards you? If so, then fair enough. If not, then what does it matter? You can't be responsible for everyone's opinions, only your own.

'When you are offended at any one's fault, turn at once to yourself and consider of what similar fault you yourself are guilty; such as esteeming for good things, money, pleasure, a little glory, or the like. By fixing your attention on this you will speedily forget your anger, especially if it occurs to you that he acts under compulsion and cannot do otherwise.'

Marcus Aurelius, *Meditations*, X, 30

Marcus Aurelius presents here another way of dealing with hurt feelings. How often does our anger hide our own vanity and hypocrisy? Are we not also guilty of similar misjudgements, irrational impulses or petty motivations? Realizing this will help you not only to overcome your hurt, but also to forgive the person whose thoughtless or selfish behaviour has offended you.

for revenge). Mental pain is an inner experience of something unwelcome, such as envy, grief and jealousy (the Stoics would also include pity as a negative emotion, though – owing to the West's cultural debt to Christianity – we might not see this as wholly negative). And mental pleasure, which is a positive response to something welcome, such as joy, love, delight and so on.

From ancient Greece onwards, through the medieval scholasticism of St Thomas Aquinas (1225–1274) to the more scientifically based rationalism of René Descartes, numerous philosophers have attempted to provide a categorization of feelings and emotions, and have differed on various points. But for our purposes it doesn't much matter whether you agree with the Stoic's precise classification; the main thing is that you understand the potentially disruptive role that certain strong feelings can play.

So, what can we do about them? We should underline here that the Stoics did not consider all emotions to be bad. If we think of passion as feeling turned up to 11, then it is also possible for certain feelings to have positive functions when dialled down to more manageable levels. Many Stoics praised the positive role of affection and cheerfulness in our daily dealings with others, and even the negative feelings of caution or wariness (a dilution of fear, perhaps). But the point about all of them, even in their mild form, is that they may lead to potentially false judgements. Since our soul/mind contains both rational and irrational elements, there's no such thing as a pure emotion or thought; emotion *colours* and influences everything we think.

Take an example: if you fear that you might not make your rent this month (a rational fear, you might think), whether you do or not, you forget the deeper and broader sense in which there is *actually nothing to fear*. This may be barren consolation when a month or two later you find yourself living on the street in a cardboard box (or a barrel, maybe ...?), but this is Stoicism's bottom line: *nothing can hurt the truly virtuous person*. The things we fear the loss of, or which form the basis for jealousy, grief or anger, were only ever ours on loan. The cure for these unpleasant feelings is, therefore, to strip away our concept of ourselves down to the bare bones – the absolute necessities – and to see all feelings as a sort of mistaken evaluation. This seems like a hard lesson, but – the Stoic would point out – better that than the harder lesson that Fate itself may eventually deal us.

One of the chief culprits here is pleasure, which often provides a false gloss upon those things we desire. While Stoics considered pleasure in general to be an irrational force, and therefore to be distrusted, they also recognized that there is, to an extent, a 'natural' role that pleasure provides (the savour of good food, the appreciation of the natural beauty of a landscape or a face, the affection shared by true friends). But we can frequently build such things up in our minds until the mere thought of them becomes artificially supercharged with anticipations of delight and ecstasy. Such 'natural' pleasure is to 'artificial' pleasure as a nutritional diet is to fast food, or loving sex is to porn. Left to its own unregulated devices, the mind overwhelmed by passion amplifies the imagined good until it promises greater

'One man prays: "May I possess that woman!" Do you pray: "May I have no wish to possess her!" Another prays: "May I be delivered from so and so!" Pray you: "May I not need to be delivered from him!" A third cries: "May I not lose my child!" Let your prayer be: "May I not fear to lose him!" In fine, turn your prayers this way, and observe what comes out of it.'

Marcus Aurelius, *Meditations*, IX, 40

There is a modern trend of asking the universe that our desires may be manifested. And there is religious precedent for this, as we read in the gospel of Matthew: 'Ask, and it shall be given you; seek, and ye shall find; knock, and it shall be opened unto you' (7:7). It may be that Jesus had more in mind here the bestowal of spiritual gifts, rather than 'Can I please have a pony?', but whatever the case, the Stoic attitude was different. Rather than asking that our desires be fulfilled or our worries pacified, we should ask to be free from the troubling desire or fear. In this sense, Marcus views prayer as a form of meditation: that is, working on ourselves to align our feelings with the will of Fate. Only in that way can we avoid disappointment.

'Within ten days, if you return to the observance of moral principles and to the cult of reason, you will appear a God to them who now esteem you a wild beast or an ape.'

Marcus Aurelius, *Meditations*, IV, 16

I like this quote because it highlights something that we all struggle with. You make a new vow, try to implement a life change or amend a character flaw – to get your temper under control, let's say – then subsequently an upsetting event causes you to revert to old habits. You feel that you have failed. But all is not lost. You fell off the horse, that's all; and all that is required is that you get back on (return to the 'cult of reason' – your dutiful practice of rationally guided action). Forget the story of your self that you are trying to perfect, your ideas of sin or purity; in a short time, you can again be the person you want to be, for all that matters is that you are that person in the present moment. Until the next time you fall off. But you will learn to stay on for longer and longer, even if only in relation to small things. And these achievements too will get bigger.

fulfilment than its actual realization could ever provide. It is an illusion – one which, the irrational deed done, leaves behind only a sour aftertaste.

But what do we do when we feel overwhelmed, or sense the creep of unwelcome anger, lust or depression? Aside from remembering the general lesson that our feelings encourage false judgements, we should do our best to avoid, prevent or suppress the growth of the harmful passion. Your partner has left the toilet seat up (again) or done a shoddy job with the dishes; your boss continues to ignore your worthwhile contributions while favouring the pretty young new recruit; your racist auntie has again outlined her strident views on asylum seekers … you get the idea. Whatever flicks your switch, then try to anticipate that, and prepare a more considered response. Take deep breaths. Count to ten. As members of Alcoholics Anonymous are encouraged to identify those triggers that may cause a relapse into old negative patterns of behaviour, so we *feelaholics* must guard against anger, grief, lust, envy or despair. By nipping them in the bud, we can redirect our thoughts down healthier channels and remind ourselves that we have no legitimate *reason* to feel that way – and how much better we will feel if we don't.

None of which should imply that the Stoics were killjoys. For all of their intense opposition to the teachings of Epicurus, Stoicism shared his simple belief that moderation was best. We need not eradicate emotion or pleasure – in fact, we cannot – but we can tame them so that they serve, instead of undermine, a rational and calm sense of how to deal with the ups and downs of life.

'The cause of anger is the belief that we are injured; this belief, therefore, should not be lightly entertained. We ought not to fly into a rage even when the injury appears to be open and distinct: for some false things bear the semblance of truth. We should always allow some time to elapse, for time discloses the truth.'

Seneca, *On Anger*, XXII

Here we see Seneca's analysis of the various stages of anger, and the importance of initial impressions, that first irrational impulse we cannot control. We have the 'injury', then we have the belief that we are injured, and then the conclusion that we are justified in feeling angry. But in such cases, were we to take the time to consider the nature of the injury, we would find that we are not injured at all – only our pride or our vanity. The remedy for this is time, to create a space between that first instinctual temptation to feel offended, and the judgement that justifies that. Creating that space between irrational response and rational judgement is fundamental to Stoicism – and to your development of yourself.

THINK ABOUT...

Remember that the Stoics believed that the only things that are within our control is our judgements. Beauty, wealth, status, talent – all are ultimately out of our hands. Yes, we might try to acquire or hang on to these preferred indifferents, but even if you are at birth gifted them, at any time Fortune could whip them away. So, we should learn to be indifferent to them. The key to all this is how you deal with your feelings.

Seneca provides a useful analysis. When bad things happen to us, there is an initial point where we first become aware of how we feel about something. Someone steps on your foot, calls you ugly, runs off with your boyfriend, insults your dog – but *before* you are overcome with annoyance/hurt/jealousy/fury (delete as appropriate), there is a small window within which you can assess what you think about what has just happened. *This* is the moment of judgement. What do you think when your complete collection of Disney-themed plushies goes up in flames after your cat knocked over a candle that your wife had forgotten to extinguish? Well, you will probably think many things. But really, the only one that matters is: have you been truly harmed?

Assuming you were not hurt in the fire, the answer is probably 'no'; and even if you were, the answer is still likely 'no', because Stoicism only recognizes one type of harm: the injury to your potential happiness. And here, the good news is that there is no such thing. For those things that are in your control are also immune to harm; that is, your state of mind.

So, to return to Seneca's point, following that initial impression, you may assess the situation and realize that, actually, those plushies were only a temporary possession; even the burns sustained by your foolish attempts to rescue plushy Princess Jasmine, at least, are not technically 'harm', in the fullest Stoic sense. So, adjusting your mindset by reasoning through your relationship with what you have lost, you are able to ward off the sort of mental pain that most plushy-loving people might feel in your position.

The ability to act this way takes practice, and the bigger the loss – career, home, family, loved ones – the harder it is to achieve. This is why Seneca recommends that you practise your response to various misfortunes, so that when they do happen, you will be in a better place to deal with them. Of course, the object is not to be blasé about the loss – the response of someone watching their entire family killed in a flash flood should not be to shrug and say '*C'est la vie*'. We are, and always will be, human, and our natural reactions are part of that. But it will help us to weather the worst of the upset if we can rehearse the sort of judgements we should make when such misfortunes befall us.

Another useful point here is made by Chrysippus, choosing a metaphor no doubt based on his own experience as a long-distance runner. Passion, he says, is like a person running at full tilt; the sprinter cannot simply come to an immediate stop. Similarly, then, to be in the throes of grief or anger or desire is the wrong point at which to start reasoning with yourself. Reason has already been overwhelmed and – while obviously you should still try to restrain yourself

– the horse has already bolted. Better, then, to wait until you have calmed down and then – before it happens the next time – think how you would prefer to react. Given time, we may train ourselves to nip anger, grief or desire in the bud – when it is only just starting to walk, as it were, and before it picks up pace.

GOING FURTHER...

1. Remember the little period of time I asked you to try to carve out for yourself every day back in the very first exercise (see page 30)? That too is a form of meditation, a period for calm reflection. So, as an alternative to adopting some form of Buddhism, mindfulness or some more defined practice, you could expand on this reflective period by simply acknowledging each thought and worry as it arises, and reminding yourself that many of these things – that row with your brother, your wayward teenager, whether or not you keep your job – are (despite your best efforts) ultimately out of your control. Then simply park it: do not look for solutions or try to engage with it, just put it on a shelf with your other concerns. It has not gone away – you are not trying to smother it or giving up on resolving the problem – but for just this moment you have acknowledged its existence, and it is now no longer thumping at the door, demanding to be let in. Once you have done this, move on to the next worry. Eventually, you may find your mind becoming calmer and clearer. Emotions and worries are like children having tantrums; frequently all they want is attention. Acknowledge them, then let them burn out on their own.

2. I can't ask you to deliberately stub your toe or smack your funny bone on the stair banister, but being mindful of those little triggers that commonly 'set you off' is a good way to begin to get your feelings under control. To reiterate, the point is not to suppress or deny those feelings, but rather to create a little gap between reflex and reason, between impulse and judgement. The more we do this and try to make it a mental habit to pause (literally, count to ten, if it helps), then the more it will become a second nature. (As I type this, the cat nudged my elbow and spilt my tea, then mewed for food – at which I patiently acknowledged her hunger and politely enquired whether she too had a book to write – yes, let's say that was my response ...).

3. Let's go a bit deeper into the distinction between what I have termed 'natural' and 'artificial' pleasures. You can apply this to almost anything. I have mentioned sex and food, which are the most obvious ones, but pleasure can ally with fantasy to create a heightened sense of desire for a wide range of things – a new film, book or computer game; an upcoming holiday; a job or duty that isn't the one to which you are currently committed. We looked at this in one of the exercises in chapter 4,

when we analysed happiness (see page 85). But of course, the opposite is also true: our imaginations can make us dread things that turn out not to be so bad. Here I want you to have a think about something you are particularly dreading – a dentist's appointment, a difficult conversation, an upcoming work assignment – and try to divest the nightmare from the reality. Set aside what you imagine will happen (the lack of pleasure or enjoyment) and try to feel what it will be like when you are there, based on previous or similar experiences. Does it help?

LOVE

WHY BEING NATURAL IS THE KEY
TO ALL RELATIONSHIPS

9

What does 'love' mean to you?

There are, of course, different types: romantic and sexual love, for one's spouse or partner; filial love, between a parent and child; the deep affection fostered between close friends; the patriotic love of one's country or culture; the spiritual or devotional love of God; even a love of one's work or the pursuit of some ideal. That we can think of all these as forms of love suggests that they have something in common, which is more or less what the Stoics thought. We share with the animals an instinctive love for our offspring, and such natural impulses are at the root of our desire to bond, protect and take pleasure in the people and things we love. From this, we may develop and train this impulse so that it forms the basis of higher and more sophisticated feelings.

This is perhaps most clearly expressed by Hierocles (*fl.* second century AD), who argued that we each find ourselves at the centre of a series of concentric circles. This is based on an idea known as *oikeiōsis*, which seems to originate with Zeno, and which may be roughly translated as 'affiliation', but basically means 'our sense of what belongs to us'. Instinctively, within the smallest circle, we care for our own self first and foremost, but gradually as we grow, the boundary encircling those things we care about starts to broaden – our sense of 'affiliation' widens to include our family, our friends, our community, the people of our country, of other countries and eventually the whole world.

A similar idea can also be found in Plato's *Symposium*, which involves a debate on the nature of Eros, the Greek god of love, and the different forms that he may take. In that dialogue, Socrates recounts the teachings of Diotima of Mantinea (*fl.* fifth century BC), a priestess and philosopher who had taught him her ideas on love. She had said that, although 'erotic' love focuses on sensual, even selfish enjoyment, it has the potential to expand infinitely. We begin with sexual attraction to an individual, and the love of that person's beautiful body, and from there to the appreciation of such physical beauty in others. But from our love of the physically beautiful individual, we may also come to love the beauty of their personality or character, the beauty of their ideas, and from there the beautiful characters and personal qualities of others also. And so, gradually, we broaden and evolve our concept of beauty, making it more abstract and refined, until we come eventually to the divine and perfect idea of beauty itself (what Plato called its 'Form'). This is the idea behind the common notion of Platonic love ('Oh, no,

'Everything has two handles: one by which it may be borne, another by which it cannot. If your brother acts unjustly, do not lay hold on the affair by the handle of the injustice, for by that it cannot be borne, but rather by the opposite – that he is your brother, that he was brought up with you; and thus you will lay hold on it as it is to be borne.'

Epictetus, *Enchiridion*, XLIII

It seems, at first, that what Epictetus is asking for here is special consideration or bias – that we go lighter on those with whom we have some bond. But that's not it at all. He wants us to see another's wrongdoing towards us with compassion, as the actions of another fallible human. In this instance, what makes us temper our feelings of hurt is our bond to our brother – our shared upbringing, our love for him. It is because we know and love him that we can forgive him. But the same should apply to everyone: we are all fallible humans, there are always two sides to every story, and although we may not condone, we may forgive. For everyone is our 'brother'.

'When [Zeno] was asked
what a friend was, he
replied, "Another I".'

Zeno of Citium, quoted in Diogenes Laërtius,
The Lives and Opinions of Eminent Philosophers, VII, 19

Friendship was highly prized among the Greek philosophers.
Epicurus, Plato and Aristotle all celebrated it – in fact,
according to Diogenes Laërtius, when asked the same
question, Aristotle is said to have replied, 'One soul abiding
in two bodies' (V, 11), which is essentially Zeno's point. A true
friend is someone whom we value as much as ourselves, and
therefore someone whose opinions and advice we can trust
– because they care as much for us as for themselves.

we're not going out – we're just Platonic'), but as you can see, this is rather underselling the term!

It may be that Plato's account of Diotima's concept of the 'ladder of love', as it has been called, was an influence on Hierocles, but whatever the case, we can see that what he was suggesting was a similar process. No matter its origin, sexual and sensual, animalistic or erotic, love was capable of great development and could therefore serve as the bond that united a couple, a family, a community, a country and even the whole of humanity. The Stoic emphasis on 'being natural' played a positive role in their concept of human relations. This is interesting when we contrast it with those who would argue for a sort of Social Darwinism. This was a moral theory prevalent in the nineteenth century, associated with such thinkers as Herbert Spencer (1820–1903) and Francis Galton (1822–1911), but which also had an influence on writers such as HG Wells (1866–1946) and Aldous Huxley (1894–1963), although both recognized its dystopian potential. The theory presents the general idea that we should base our moral code on the doctrines of natural selection and the survival of the fittest as evidenced in Darwinism: those who survive and thrive have been 'selected' by nature to succeed. The theory fell out of favour along with the demise of National Socialism, but lately seems to be making a comeback in political and economic circles, where, for some reason, the idea that the rich *naturally* deserve their wealth (and the poor deserve their lack of it) has come to have a certain appeal ...

However, as Hierocles and Diotima illustrate, admitting our 'naturalness' need not lead us towards the idea that 'might is right' and it is perfectly fine to lighten the sled by leaving granny behind on the ice floe to fend off the wolves on her own. As pointed out by anarchist philosopher Peter Kropotkin (1842–1921), there is as much evidence in nature to support the view that life on earth is based on cooperation and mutual assistance as there is to suggest that it is 'a war of each against all', to reference the rather pessimistic view of English philosopher Thomas Hobbes (1588–1679).

While they were at odds on other things, the Stoics shared with Epicurus an emphasis on the importance of friendship. A good friend is someone who appreciates your character, would tell you painful truths (if necessary) and generally wants you to be the best you can be. Epictetus considered that sexual or romantic passion is likely to lead us astray and that there should be no sex before marriage, but we should instead look to cultivate a general love for humanity and to consider all people our brothers and sisters. Similarly, Marcus Aurelius counselled that, while avoiding the extremes of emotional excitement, we should try instead to be cheerful and affectionate in our daily dealings with one another.

Judging from the above, you may be tempted to detect here the influence upon Stoicism of Christianity, but actually the debt goes the other way and it is the doctrines of Stoicism – especially the views of Epictetus – upon which Christianity drew as it grew and developed, as well as those of Plato, whose views on non-sexual love were also later drafted in to bolster the notion of Christian *agápē*, the unconditional love between God and humanity, and the love of one's neighbour as oneself.

But what about romantic relationships? We may detect in some Stoics a certain indifference to romantic attachment, even perhaps hostility. Love is a passion, remember (or at least, it can be), and so should be avoided. This not only meant a ban on extra- and pre-marital sex, but also a prohibition against the excesses of romantic love in general. That said, certain Stoics do have plenty of positive things to say about marriage. Marcus Aurelius praises the loyalty, friendship and support of his wife Faustina (despite some unsubstantiated rumours, they seem to have been devoted to each other). We may also cite Antipater of Tarsus, whose work *On Marriage* saw matrimony as the basis of civil order but also essential to human happiness, and in doing so challenged the prevalent view of women as inferior (he seems to have originated the term 'misogyny'). This is a view also shared by Gaius Musonius Rufus, who made the case that women were as equally equipped to study philosophy as men.

Admittedly, this view of matrimonial love is not exactly the stuff of *Romeo and Juliet*, but these were also times when marriage was seen in more transactional terms for both parties, often used to cement political allegiances or to produce heirs. This doesn't mean that Stoicism was 'anti' romantic love, but rather emphasized that what endures between partners must be more than simply physical attraction and should avoid the extremes of erotic passion.

'Each of us is, as it were, circumscribed by many circles; some of which are less, but others larger, and some comprehend, but others are comprehended, according to the different and unequal habitudes with respect to each other. For the first, indeed, and most proximate circle is that which every one describes about his own mind as a centre, in which circle the body, and whatever is assumed for the sake of the body, are comprehended. For this is nearly the smallest circle, and almost touches the centre itself. The second from this, and which is at a greater distance from the centre, but comprehends the first circle, is that in which parents, brothers, wife, and children are arranged. The third circle from the centre is that which contains uncles and aunts, grandfathers and grandmothers, and the children of brothers and sisters. After this is the circle which comprehends the remaining relatives. Next to this is that which contains the common people, then that which comprehends those of the same tribe, afterwards that

which contains the citizens; and then two other circles follow, one being the circle of those that dwell in the vicinity of the city, and the other, of those of the same province. But the outermost and greatest circle, and which comprehends all the other circles, is that of the whole human race.'

Hierocles, 'How we ought to conduct ourselves towards our kindred', quoted in Stobaeus, *Florilegium*, IV

Here Hierocles makes the same point as Epictetus, but via the analogy of concentric circles, increasing in size outwards from the self, and each of which 'comprehends' (includes) the previous one. Beginning with our own concern for our body, our sense of 'what belongs to us' (*oikeiōsis*), and moving outwards until it eventually incorporates all of humanity.

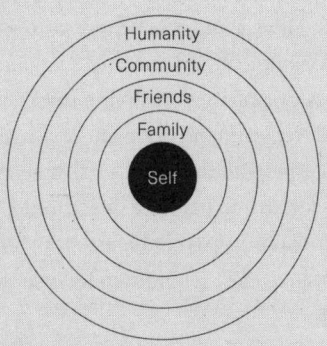

THINK ABOUT...

For the Stoics, then, love is a natural instinct that binds us all together. It may begin selfishly, through a concern for self-preservation, but expands to include offspring, family, one's community, and beyond that a commitment to broader social concerns, humanitarian ideals and charitable causes.

The problem most of us face in matters of love is that they often stir up negative emotions. Drawing upon and developing existing Greek concepts, Christianity divided love into four main types: *érōs* (sexual love), *storgē* (parental and familial love), *philía* (love for one's friends) and *agápē* (unconditional love for God and one's fellow humans). As you can see, apart from *agápē*, all the other forms involve potential conflict. Sexual desire can lead to lust, deviancy, jealousy and envy; familial relations between children and parents can lead to grief, betrayal, coercion, resentment; even friendship or a feeling of communal belonging can create rifts and internal disputes, or animosity towards those we consider 'other' or outside our group or tribe. It is only selfless universal love that avoids these issues.

Stoicism does not quite have an equivalent of Christian *agápē* – there is no spiritual or divine love – but as we have seen, they did recommend a form of universal brother/sisterhood or *cosmopolitanism*. They also agreed that, while erotic love is a natural instinct, we should guard against inflaming it into an uncontrollable passion. So, we might say that the sort of love they recommended was a broad type of

'It is man's special business to love even those who err; and to this love you attain, if it is borne in upon you that even these sinners are your kin, and that they offend through ignorance and against their will.'

Marcus Aurelius, *Meditations*, VII, 22

Here, like Epictetus (see page 159), we see Marcus appealing to kinship as the basis for forgiveness, although here the reason for this kinship is slightly different, for he goes on to say that we are all human and therefore equally mortal. Like Plato and Socrates, he argues that wrongdoing is based on ignorance. The use of 'sin' here is just a quirk of the translation, but there are indeed religious parallels to this sentiment, as in Luke 23:34, where, as Jesus is being crucified, the Roman soldiers cast lots for his clothes: 'Father, forgive them;' he says, 'for they know not what they do.' But religious or secular, the essential point is that each of us acts according to what we think is for the best, and we must recognize in others' moral failure our own common fallibility.

philía, where we try to expand our concern for those around us to include as many people as possible.

Applying this in more practical terms, we may break it down into two main concerns: controlling the passions and eradicating prejudice. We must guard against the power of erotic love to overwhelm our reason and will, and we must try to extend our concern beyond the borders of our own family, tribe and nation.

Let us take sexual love first. Perhaps the most common negative emotion related to this is jealousy. You fear that your partner may run off with someone else. How would a Stoic respond to this? It was Sting (not, as far as I know, a Stoic, but I believe he has some Buddhist leanings) who sang, 'If you love somebody set them free'. The Stoics would agree. As with all other 'possessions', your loved one does not truly belong to you. They are a gift from the universe, but even more so than a house or a car, they have their own free will (sort of ...). And so, to quote William Blake ('Eternity'):

He who binds to himself a joy
Does the winged life destroy
He who kisses the joy as it flies
Lives in eternity's sunrise

In all other erotic respects, the key is self-control or moderation. As with hunger or thirst, sex is an appetite that must be ruled by reason. It has its natural place and limits, and also illegitimate forms of expression that go beyond that. So, you should not blame yourself for your natural and sometimes counter-rational urges, but you must hold yourself responsible for whether or not you act on them.

The other, social aspect of love concerns how far we extend it. Modern society is hyper-aware of these issues, and so will you be. In terms of how we treat people, we should not discriminate in our treatment of people based on their race, gender, sexual orientation, nationality, class, religion or other what are often called 'protected characteristics'. The Stoics would broadly agree with this, though we should also note that the world of ancient Greece and Rome was not particularly egalitarian or liberal, and was riven with prejudice concerning sex roles, status, nationality and class. Everyone outside of classical culture was considered a 'barbarian', and of course both societies were built on slavery. All I can say in defence is that those were different times, and that the principles of Stoicism are not tied to the characteristics of the societies in which it was practised. However, today's Stoics need not be constrained by such prejudices, and Stoicism's view of humanity as a single community is a timely inspiration for us all to strive towards a more loving and inclusive world.

'I also think that a married life is beautiful. For what other thing can be such an ornament to a family, as is the association of husband and wife? For it must not be said that sumptuous edifices, walls covered with marble plaster, and piazzas adorned with stones, which are admired by those who are ignorant of true good, nor yet paintings and arched myrtle walks, nor any thing else which is the subject of astonishment to the stupid, is the ornament of a family. But the beauty of a household consists in the conjunction of man and wife, who are united to each other by destiny, and are consecrated to the Gods who preside over nuptials, births, and houses, and who accord, indeed, with each other, and have all things in common, as far as to their bodies, or rather their souls themselves.'

Hierocles, 'On wedlock', quoted in Stobaeus, *Florilegium*, IV

After listing the various practical advantages of marriage – the procreation of children, who will look after us when we get old; the division of domestic duties – Hierocles comes closer to modern romantic sentiments, where marriage can be seen as a sort of divinely ordained union. This underlines the fact that, although they disapproved of casual and extramarital sex, the Stoics were not puritans; they simply wanted the sexual impulse channelled in such a way that it helped build a virtuous life, not undermine it.

GOING FURTHER...

1. Take Hierocles' concentric circles and apply them to your own life. So, grab a piece of paper – a large one is best – and start with a dot representing yourself in the middle. Then draw a circle around that and add in those closest to you – the people you most care about. Then draw a bigger circle around that one and add in people you know or feel slightly less close to – perhaps friends and wider family members. Then another circle with work colleagues. Then another with casual acquaintances, people who work in your local shop or the library. Then strangers whom you know of but have never met. And then perhaps celebrities or public officials. Then people of other nations and cultures. Keep going until the widest circle includes all of humanity. Now, go back through each circle and look at the people there. What have you done for them today? What could you do to strengthen your positive ties to those in each circle?

2. Watch a nature documentary. We share something with all the world's creatures, but we are also distinct: as extraordinary as nature can be, human rationality is a quantum leap above anything the animal kingdom has to offer, and so human morality has a different basis. We don't have to abide by Darwin's 'law'. We can be compassionate,

forgiving, loving – although, as these documentaries reveal, these are not qualities that only humans possess; nature supplies the seed for what we can be. Take a moment to reflect on these commonalities and differences, what we share with our natural cousins and what is different.

3. Love and forgiveness are often mentioned together. I think this is because, if you love someone, you come to understand them, and perhaps get closer to seeing why they might have behaved in a particular way. Think of someone who has wronged you and try to put yourself in their shoes. What assumptions and motives might they have that would help you understand and forgive their actions?

EDUCATION

WHY KNOWLEDGE IS LESS
IMPORTANT THAN WISDOM

10

Having said how important wisdom is to Stoicism, I should point out that this should not be confused with intellectual knowledge.

The various schools where students in the ancient world would go to learn about philosophy might be considered forerunners of today's universities: places where young people might gather to listen to lectures, study, critique and debate. But there was no graduation ceremony or certificate to be obtained, and no strict timetable or course structure, and while some schools did charge fees, others did not. The overall aim of these institutions was, rather, to 'educate' the individual, to reform their character and outlook, which was as much a moral process as an intellectual one.

This was particularly so with Stoicism, which emphasized virtue and so put greater stress on the importance of wisdom as a guide to action and behaviour. This isn't to say that the other schools did not hold such things to be important, but they might also have emphasized logic, metaphysics or political theory. In prioritizing ethical questions and the development of personal character, Stoics cast the virtue of 'wisdom' in a different light, making intellect serve action.

So, how did they define wisdom? It is still common today to distinguish wisdom from knowledge or information. An *informed* person may *know* that it is not forecast to rain this afternoon; a *wise* person has learnt still to pack an umbrella, because it doesn't always pay to trust the weather forecast. There is a sense here that wisdom is applied knowledge, or knowledge that has been filtered and vetted by experience. This is also true of Stoic wisdom: we become wise when we see what role knowledge can play in our lives. It is all very well to *know* that the passions are dangerous, but another thing to fully understand in what way they harm us and what we can do to avoid their influence. Wisdom, for the Stoics, was therefore often *phrónēsis,* the practical knowledge of how to live, which was based on *sophia,* our broader and deeper philosophical understanding of the true nature of life – from whence, of course, we get 'philosophy': the love (*philo*) of wisdom (*sophia*).

Other ancient philosophers shared this view. For instance, Aristotle also considered *phrónēsis* to be the know-how that

'The reason why we have two
ears and only one mouth is
that we may listen the more
and talk the less.'

Zeno of Citium, quoted in Diogenes Laërtius,
The Lives and Opinions of Eminent Philosophers, VII, 19

As a practical philosophy, Stoicism naturally emphasizes the
importance of action over speech. Zeno could be especially
harsh on his own pupils, and this particular putdown was
directed at a young man whom he considered to be spouting
copious nonsense. This reinforces the point that philosophy
(and Stoicism especially) is not concerned with the
trappings of knowledge – scoring debating points, getting
qualifications or looking clever in front of your mates – but
with acquiring an understanding that can be of practical
benefit in helping us to live 'the good life'.

'What is the first business of him who philosophizes? To throw away self-conceit. For it is impossible for a man to begin to learn that which he thinks that he knows.'

Epictetus, *Discourses*, II, 17

This wonderful quote reminds me of a Zen Buddhist parable, where the teacher is pouring a cup of tea for his student. When the tea reaches the top of the cup, the teacher continues to pour, causing the student to point this out. 'It's a bit like you, isn't it?' says the teacher. Here Epictetus makes the same point: 'education' can often be as much about *unlearning* as it is about acquiring new knowledge. The old beliefs have to be reassessed and, if necessary, thrown out, before anything new can take their place.

we acquire through experience as to the correct application of courage, moderation and other virtues, and therefore an essential component of the ethical life. Stoics didn't believe in Aristotle's 'middle way', where an ethical action was often the midpoint between extremes of behaviour, because for them, everything was fairly black and white. There wasn't 'just the right amount' of love for money, because such concerns were neither matters of virtue nor vice, but rather indifferent to the moral life, and therefore (while we might be naturally inclined to prefer some of them), ultimately inessential to it. This didn't mean that there was nothing to learn, or no debate to be had about *how* the virtues should be applied, but the general emphasis was on this black-and-white distinction between the things that were truly good (or bad), and those things that were neither (indifferent or neutral). This led some Stoics to argue that 'all sins are equal', because you're either virtuous or you aren't – which seems a bit hardline, as if murder was no worse than stealing paperclips from the office stationery cupboard! But maybe they were just saying this for rhetorical effect. In any case, to sum up, Stoic wisdom consisted in knowing that all but our mental judgements are outside of our control, and that peace of mind can only be obtained through acceptance of this and through cultivating an indifference to money, pleasure, status and other indifferents.

Returning to the comparison between ancient and modern education, we can see a significant difference. There is no explicit moral component to a modern university-level education, and no deliberate intention to make you a better person (unless you are training to be a priest or a therapist, perhaps). This is true even of modern philosophy courses, which are more often concerned with highly abstract debates and theoretical analysis than imbuing you with a better moral compass. This is not to romanticize ancient philosophical schools, some of which – such as the Sophists – were solely dedicated to the more 'practical' art of teaching students how to win at all costs (and a modern equivalent of which might be today's law schools). Such 'graduates' were similarly concerned with being furnished with the tools to acquire the very sort of goods (money, status, power) that the Stoics frowned upon. But I think it is also fair to say that education today is generally more concerned with the accumulation of socially useful facts and skills.

Having said all this, it is only fair to point out that the lack of a moral or spiritual component in most forms of modern education is a deliberate choice. It assumes that the primary job of teachers is to equip students with a broad range of skills and knowledge with which they can then make their own choices – about what to believe and what sort of person to be. It is, therefore, an expression of democratic freedom.

But whatever the failings or narrow focus of this education, the upshot is that most of us leave it (at whatever level) with a sort of gap in our *life skills*. To return to the terms of the Greek philosophers, we are encouraged to acquire *epistēmē* (theoretical knowledge) and *technē* (technical knowledge), but we lack *sophia* (a deeper understanding of life) and *phrónēsis* (practical ethical and psychological know-how). As a result, anyone looking to fill that gap will need

'Who then makes improvement? Is it he who has read many books of Chrysippus? But does virtue consist in having understood Chrysippus?'

Epictetus, *Discourses*, I, 4

Epictetus is speaking here of moral progress or self-improvement. If someone considers that to lie in having read a lot of philosophy (such as the works of Chrysippus), then this would mean that self-improvement is different to virtue, for simply reading a lot of books doesn't make you virtuous. No, it lies in doing the work. 'And where is your work?' Epictetus continues. 'In desire and in aversion.' In other words, it is in acquiring true knowledge of good and bad, what to seek and what to shun, and actively employing that understanding in daily affairs.

'The Gods watched over me also when I first applied myself to philosophy. For I fell not into the hands of any Sophist, nor sat poring over many volumes, nor devoted myself to solving syllogisms, or star-gazing.'

Marcus Aurelius, *Meditations*, I, 17

As previously mentioned, the first book of Marcus's *Meditations* is basically a 'thank you' list, in which he itemizes his many debts – to his teachers, family members and the gods themselves – for their role in making him the person he has become (see page 102). We can see here that chief among these gratitudes is that he was not distracted into what he considered to be more trivial philosophical pursuits – fruitless intellectual controversies and the sort of 'logic chopping' that some schools favoured – or the unscrupulous methods of the Sophists, who, as I've mentioned, were basically philosophers-for-hire and would teach you how to win any argument, by fair means or foul. A little earlier on, for similar reasons, he is also grateful that he 'made no greater progress in rhetoric and poetry', all of which meant that he was able to concentrate on the central questions of life: how to be a good and happy person. As for 'star gazing', I assume he means astrology here, but it could also be astronomy, or even just dreamily admiring the night's sky (to write poems about, perhaps), all of which are less urgent and meaningful pursuits than the knowledge of oneself.

to do so under their own steam. But how? Well, by books like this, of course, and other forms of reading and self-study – I encourage you to check out the 'Further Reading' and 'Sources' sections, which list some useful places to start (see pages 230–233). But it is still a daunting task. There are so many belief systems, religions, philosophies, therapies and so on, each one making a strident claim for its being the right one for you. How do you choose?

There is something to be said for trial and error – you can't make an omelette without cracking a few eggs. But perhaps a better indication is to look for a viewpoint's practical benefits. Christianity tells us that 'ye shall know them by their fruits' (Matthew 7:16), which simply means: are those who promote a certain philosophy or way of life *themselves* a good advert for it? When we ask this question of the Stoics, we find that they generally are. There are documented acts of heroism, compassion, courage in adversity and calm fortitude. By contemporary accounts, many of them seemed happy and virtuous. So, when weighing up what to believe, or which path to follow, we should perhaps think less about the various doctrines and dogmas that a certain outlook professes – its theoretical and technical knowledge – and focus more on the wisdom that allowed its practitioners to live a meaningful and happy life.

THINK ABOUT...

How much of your knowledge and education has helped you to become a better or a happier person? It is a question for which even students of philosophy and psychology may find themselves surprised by their answer. Epictetus queried the value of purely intellectual pursuits, even when applied to Stoicism. Do we judge a person's virtue by the number of Chrysippus's books that they've read? It would be like asking a wrestler to show us his strength, and he points to the weights he uses to train. The same thing applies to intellectual knowledge: we don't want to know how well read you are, but what you have learnt and applied from the knowledge you have acquired through your reading. It is like the relationship between diet and exercise: it is all very well loading up on the right calories, but unless you actually do something with them, then all you will get is fat.

Cultural doomsayers have long been bemoaning the adverse effect of technology: the advent of mobile phones and social media, the growth of 'text speak' and the damage it is doing to spelling and grammar. Bookshops and publishers wring their hands at the irreversible decline in novel reading – and book reading in general – where a 2023 poll from *The Economist*/YouGov found that almost half of Americans read no books at all that year.

But perhaps such statistics distort the situation. Human literacy is now the highest it has ever been in world history – almost ninety per cent, and a complete inversion from two hundred years ago, where barely ten per cent were literate. And people are reading all the time – blogs, posts and online news articles, emails, texts and tweets (or whatever they are called now). They are also listening to podcasts, watching videos and TikToks, and following increasingly convoluted long-form serial television – and if you have ever listened to a teenager recap off-the-cuff the whole eight seasons of *Game of Thrones*, then you will have no anxiety about dropping attention spans, comprehension deficit or reduced memory retention. We live in a media-saturated world. There is now just so much *stuff* – which, of course, brings its own concerns. For how much of it is actually good for you?

As Epictetus pointed out, information in itself is not enough to make you happy or virtuous. You must process it, work on it, apply it to your life. You can paste up as many motivational quotes as you want, read as many popular philosophy books as your relatives will gift you, but unless you sit down with yourself and seriously consider how to utilize all this information, then what use is it?

Instead of studying books, Stoicism advises us to study *ourselves*. Of course, we may do this in any number of ways – and there is no reason that reading or education can't form a part of that process of self-reflection (and in fact, following a course or working through a book can be a good way of setting aside dedicated time to work on yourself). As Marcus Aurelius did in his *Meditations*, you also need to observe yourself and analyse your motives and your attitudes, your assumptions and your biases. Only through this sort of active reflection will you spot your bad habits, your trigger points and your lazy thinking. Stoicism is not a badge to be worn or a source of quotes with which you can spice up your dinner conversation or your dating game. It is a manual for living.

'The condition and characteristic of a vulgar person is that he never looks for either help or harm from himself, but only from externals. The condition and characteristic of a philosopher is that he looks to himself for all help or harm.'

Epictetus, *Enchiridion*, XLVIII

'Vulgar' here simply means 'common' or 'average', the person in the street as opposed to the philosopher. But most of us do it: we blame others, or seek external help for our problems, when the answer lies 'within us' – in the attitudes that we adopt to our own troubles. If we spent more time studying ourselves, then we wouldn't need books – apart from *this* one, of course ...

GOING FURTHER...

1. Whatever level of formal education you have, take a moment to think about what it has contributed to your life – I mean, aside from allowing you to get a job or to qualify you for the study of yet higher qualifications. What have you *learnt*, about life or yourself? If you have one, dig out an old school report. What sort of things did your teachers value? Are 'talkative' or 'tendency to daydream' really such bad qualities, Mr Protheroe? Did the things you were praised for, or which you were good at, make a difference to *you*, as a person? Did they make you *virtuous*, in the Stoic sense?

2. Having done the above exercise, now reverse it: think about those personal qualities, virtues, pieces of wisdom or life lessons that you do consider yourself to possess. Where did they come from? Your own experiences? Books? Parents or friends? TV documentaries? A mixture of all of these things? Where might you find more? Where are you lacking?

3. Finally, look at your bookshelves or DVD collection (do you still have one?). What are your favourite books or films or plays? Have they changed over time? Do you still rate that story you loved when you were younger? For those

you do, what lasting 'lessons' do you think they left you with? Fiction forms us as much as (perhaps more than) formal types of education, but its values and beliefs are often smuggled in. Pick a single book or film (or whatever) and try to unpack its message. Do you still share that? The overall point of these three exercises is to get you to critically assess where any 'wisdom' you have acquired has actually come from. Certainly, not all of it will have come from formal education, even if its stated aim was to deliver some sort of ethical, spiritual or philosophical instruction. Conversely, you will also find that you have learnt valuable lessons from informal settings, from everyday experiences and events – something overheard in the street, or a joke you heard on TV. You might find that you learnt as much from *The Only Way is Essex* as you did from *The Brothers Karamazov*, or some other serious work of 'culture'. Wisdom can come from anywhere – so be open to it.

POLITICS

WHY WE HAVE A DUTY
TO ONE ANOTHER

11

It is hard to pinpoint a precise reason for the growing popularity of Stoicism.

It may be its simplicity and practical focus, which – unlike a great deal of academic philosophy – provides actionable advice that we can apply to our busy everyday lives. Or it may be its adaptability: its view of God as Nature is not as theologically laden as other forms of religion and requires little adjustment to be serviceable to a more secular, modern outlook. It may also be its emphasis on acceptance, detachment and peace of mind in a world that is constantly vying for our attention, providing concrete ways to deal with everyday ups and downs, calm the emotions and avoid the dangerous excesses of irrational passions.

In all of this, Stoicism is not hugely different, perhaps, to other forms of self-help, therapy or mindfulness, which focus on individual well-being and development. However, while this is, to an extent, true, it would be a mistake to view Stoicism solely as a form of personal salvation.

Aristotle believed that humans are 'political animals', in that we are inclined by our natures to be communal (that is, to live in a *polis*, which was the Greek term for the sort of small city state that Aristotle believed to be the ideal form of community). The Stoics seem to have shared a similar view, believing that we are inherently social beings, who naturally form communities in order to support and rely on one another. Unlike Epicureanism, which concerns itself primarily with personal happiness, Stoicism believes that we have a moral duty to contribute towards the well-being of others and the common good.

If we look back through the prominent Stoics, aside from Marcus Aurelius (an emperor) and Seneca (a politician), we find many that were politically and socially active. Asked by King Antigonus II Gonatus (*c.*320–239 BC) to come to Macedonia to act as his adviser, Zeno declined, but sent in his stead his pupils Philonides and Persaeus, who would go on to serve the king well. Sphaerus (*c.*285–*c.*221 BC), another of Zeno's pupils, would go on to influence political reform in Sparta under their king Cleomenes III (*c.*265–219 BC). We may add to this such figures as Gaius Blossius (*fl.* second century BC), Panaetius, Athenodorus Cananites (*c.*74 BC–AD 7) and Thrasea Paetus (*d.* AD 66), all of whom played active roles

'What profits not the swarm profits not the bee.'

Marcus Aurelius, *Meditations*, VI, 54

This is about the common good. Marcus seems particularly taken with the beehive analogy for society – it occurs elsewhere in the *Meditations* and was also used by other classical writers, such as by Virgil in his *Georgics* and Aristotle in his *History of Animals*. The idea is that selfish people have it backward: if our self-interested actions ultimately harm (or at least do not profit) society, then this will rebound back upon us – because we rely on society. And so, we pay taxes because we use roads, hospitals, education; we help others, because at some point someone else will help us. This is not communism or socialism, but simple common sense: we are all interconnected and interdependent.

in the politics of their day. When Greece wished to send a political envoy to Rome in 155 BC to appeal the size of a fine that had been levied against them, they sent their best philosophers – among them Diogenes of Babylon, then head of the Stoic school and whose eloquence was responsible for the burgeoning Roman interest in Stoicism. Helvidius Priscus (*fl.* first century AD) was also a passionate republican, who worked courageously to oppose the growing imperial abuses of power and was eventually banished and put to death for it by Emperor Vespasian (AD 9–79). In fact, at various points in his reign, Emperor Domitian (AD 51–96) considered the threat of philosophers so great that he had them all banished from Rome, and even the whole of the Italian peninsula! Hard to think of that happening now – or that anyone would see any benefit in doing so.

All of that said, there isn't any official 'Stoic political philosophy', as there is with Marxism, for instance. Chrysippus and Zeno (as we shall see) did conjecture about the form of the ideal society, but mostly we have Stoics who happen to be politicians and who then apply their Stoic values in their political dealings. This is fitting: as a form of virtue ethics, Stoicism focuses on teaching the individual how to be virtuous, then leaves it up to that individual to apply that virtue to whatever context they find themselves in.

To illustrate this difference of approach, we may compare two *Republics*, that of Stoicism's founder Zeno, and the more famous one of Plato. Unfortunately, Zeno's text does not survive and all we know about it comes second hand, through quotations and descriptions in others' writings

'No one is able to rule unless he is also able to be ruled.'

Seneca, *On Anger*, II, 15

Seneca's point here is one made by Plato at length in various places. For instance, in *Gorgias*, Plato has Socrates argue that an immoral tyrant who may act exactly as he pleases is the most miserable of men, because he is ruled not by reason but by his own irrational desires in which he has no say. Seneca is saying the same thing: unless we are ruled by reason, we cannot have any control over ourselves. His specific focus here is anger, which he says some claim to be a 'noble' passion, such as the wrath of the lion. This applies, of course, to 'civilized' but warlike societies, who make it a point of principle to display their strength in shows of military aggression or retaliation rather than through diplomacy or peaceful policy. But, for a human being, *any* sort of passion is irrational, so how can it be noble? It is only reason that ennobles us, not passion.

(such as those of Plutarch and Diogenes Laërtius). For Zeno, there could be no top-down organization or set of rules that would determine the form of a city or community, and we must simply place our trust in human rationality and wisdom. Accordingly, he would admit no temples, law courts, *gymnasia* (schools of education) and not even any money. There would be no marriage or monogamy, so that anyone could sleep with anyone, and all child rearing would be done communally – which was also something that Plato favoured. However, whereas Zeno put faith in our inherent rationality to produce a just society, Plato was not so trusting. He argued that society functioned best if it were divided up according to 'types' of people, with the wisest (philosophers, naturally!) at the top, the bravest and most disciplined (soldiers) protecting and supporting their rule, and everyone else doing the work (farming, baking, making pots and so on). But since – presumably – people aren't *really* born to be philosophers or soldiers or farmers, but are shaped by society as such, then the rulers need to justify such divisions by a 'noble lie' that such personal characteristics and skills are indeed innate. All of which makes Zeno seem less cynical and more impractical, or Plato more realistic and more manipulative, depending on your perspective.

One feature that characterizes Zeno's ideal community – apart from the reliance upon innate rationality and goodness – is its naturalness. Zeno's advice that we must 'live in accordance with Nature', when cashed out in practical, social terms, meant that (for example) he had no hang-up about homosexuality, because that could also be observed in animal behaviour. But nor, for the same reason, did he think incest was necessarily bad (and which, if there were no 'family', as such, and everything was communal and flexible, maybe also makes a certain sort of sense – though we would now reject this for all sorts of other good reasons). Similar 'natural' arguments were advanced by Chrysippus, who also argued that there was nothing wrong with cannibalism (again, the animals did it, and what is a dead body anyway but meat?).

But before you rush off and set up your cannibalistic love commune, the key word to remember here is 'reason'. Whether you agree or not with Zeno or Chrysippus on this or that suggestion doesn't matter, because the ideal Stoic society is not based on a set of rules; it evolves through rational understanding, debate and cooperation, through trust in individuals. Possessed with the insights of modern psychology and biology, Zeno's ideal Stoic republic would likely be very different from how he initially conceived it – as would yours.

So, what does this mean for you? The bottom line is that the Stoics believed that social involvement and responsibility were a central part of life. Whether this takes the form of local activism concerning the proposed sell-off of a nearby park to property developers, or the global movement to redress the dangers of climate change, the Stoic would encourage you to be involved. For we are all part of the natural order, the single organism that encompasses the whole world, which means that your concern for the happiness and fair treatment of others needn't stop at your doorstep.

'If mind be common to us all, the reason in virtue of which we are rational is also common; so too is the power which bids us do or do not do. Therefore we have all a common law; and if so, we are fellow-citizens and members of some common polity. The Universe, then, must in a manner be a state, for of what other common polity can all mankind be said to be members?'

Marcus Aurelius, *Meditations*, IV, 4

Here Marcus is arguing that, since all people everywhere are rational beings possessing intellect and free will (in the Stoic sense), then this can act as the basis for a uniform political organization. That we share this rationality gives us something fundamental in common and makes us citizens of the same state, able to rationally agree the best laws for that state – a state which, since people everywhere have the capacity for reason, may include everyone. So, in a way, we are all citizens of the world. (The translator has chosen 'universe' here, which for Marcus was pretty much the same thing.) As he later says, 'As Antoninus [i.e. himself], my city and my country is Rome; as a human being, it is the world.' (*Meditations*, VI, 44). This beautiful ideal was later shared by the philosophers of the Enlightenment and the founding fathers of the United States of America, who also valued reason above all else (though as this attitude also resulted in the gory spectacle of the French Revolution and the Terror, we must also acknowledge that it *can* go wrong ...).

'When Vespasian sent [for Helvidius Priscus] and commanded him not to go into the senate, he replied, "It is in your power not to allow me to be a member of the senate, but so long as I am, I must go in." "Well, go in then," says the emperor, "but say nothing." "Do not ask my opinion, and I will be silent." "But I must ask your opinion." "And I must say what I think right." "But if you do, I shall put you to death." "When then did I tell you that I am immortal? You will do your part, and I will do mine: it is your part to kill; it is mine to die, but not in fear: yours to banish me; mine to depart without sorrow."'

Epictetus, *Discourses*, I, 2

The emperor Vespasian would eventually both banish Helvidius and put him to death. We can see the emperor here – in the account of Epictetus – trying to bargain with the Stoic, whose eloquence and influence in the Senate he feared. But Helvidius is having none of it: 'You do your job, and I'll do mine.' Even if that results in death. Now, your homework is: take this exchange and revise it for your next job appraisal with your boss.

THINK ABOUT...

It is easy to let the state of the world make us cynical about politics, feel powerless as to our ability to make a difference, and allow us to succumb to a sort of depressed apathy, where we try to numb ourselves with alcohol, video games and all-day binge-athons of *The Real Housewives of Beverly Hills*. Politicians also don't do themselves any favours, if I'm honest, with their penchant for sex scandals, insurrections and dodgy business practices (and that's just *one* of them ...). It's no wonder you're cynical.

But have you ever stopped to consider that perhaps you're not cynical *enough*? This is how 'they' want you to feel; if you are disengaged and apathetic, powerless and depressed, then you are less likely to actually do something that rocks the boat or challenges the status quo. And who benefits from that, eh? '*Cui bono?*' as Roman orator (and part-time Stoic) Cicero (106–43 BC) once asked. Well, that is a question for the conspiracy theorists, perhaps. But a more important question is, whose *fault* is all this? To which the simple answer is: ours. For, as the Roman satirist Juvenal (c.AD 60–c.127) noted about his own age: where once people sought military glory or high office, now they most want 'bread and circuses' (or as he might say now, Netflix and chill).

One of the key differences between Stoicism and Epicureanism is that, while Epicurus lectured from his Garden as to how we should seek happiness through moderate pleasures, Stoicism demanded that we engage with society. We can't retreat from the world in order to work on ourselves, because our fullest sense of self comes from exercising public-facing virtues, such as courage and fairness. This demands involvement and activism – whatever form that takes.

We have also seen earlier how another basis for this sense of civic duty is our natural human instincts. Our love for ourself is also the basis for our love for others, which – as Hierocles argued – can form a foundation for an ever-expanding concern for people we will likely never meet. It is *natural* for us to get involved (see pages 164–165).

Now, I should say here that this need not involve politics with a capital 'P', and nor does Stoicism prescribe what political views you should adopt. You are, of course, completely entitled to do whatever you feel inspired to do – stand for the local council, become a school governor, join a neighbourhood watch or set out on a fully fledged political career. But the point is that involvement need not involve such public acts; it merely implies that you care.

There are countless small ways in which a citizen might do this. Neighbourliness is a good one – offering to mow the lawn of the old couple who live nextdoor, or pick up their prescriptions, helping someone mend a fence or move furniture. The same obviously applies to colleagues, friends and family. You might write a letter of recommendation for your boss's niece to help with her application to university, or volunteer to help an asylum seeker deal with intimidating government bureaucracy.

The point is that 'politics' isn't always about votes, canvassing and heated debate. Acting 'politically' – that is, as a member of a *polis*, or community – is something that any one of us may do. And indeed should.

'Duties are universally measured by relations. Is a certain man your father? In this are implied taking care of him, submitting to him in all things, patiently receiving his reproaches, his correction. But he is a bad father. Is your natural tie, then, to a *good* father? No, but to a father. Is a brother unjust? Well, preserve your own just relation towards him. Consider not what *he* does, but what *you* are to do to keep your own will in a state conformable to nature, for another cannot hurt you unless you please.'

Epictetus, *Enchiridion*, XXX

There is somewhere a saying, often attributed to the Chinese sage Confucius (551–479 BC), along the lines of (and I paraphrase): if everything is right with the person, then there will be harmony in the home, order among nations and peace in the world. Epictetus is saying something similar here. If we only follow those rules we choose to, then there is a sort of butterfly effect that threatens to ripple out and unravel the fabric of society; but if we obey the small things, then the big things will look after themselves. Among those are the 'natural ties' that we have to family members. Our father or our brother may not be exemplary persons, but we must still respect their role and their kinship. I know what you want to say: but what if the father is abusive or the brother an alcoholic? Well, the Stoic will answer – as he always does – that no 'externals' can hurt you. You owe it to yourself to be a good brother or sister, son or daughter – the other things are out of your control. Of course, there are other concerns that we must bear in mind, and the key thing here is about living within the law. Epictetus doesn't say anything about not calling social services.

GOING FURTHER...

1. Get outside your filter bubble. Find a source that discusses what's currently going on in another country. What are the big stories in South Korea or Lithuania, Bolivia or Mozambique? Try to identify different concerns and controversies. Is it really true that, in Australia, it is illegal to wear pink hot pants after midday on a Sunday? Can you still not name a pig Napoleon in France? Or go back in time: what were the daily struggles of a working-class person in nineteenth-century China or seventeenth-century Egypt? Or in ancient Rome and Greece? The world is strange and diverse, as are the people that occupy it. But are there also common concerns? Reoccurring anxieties? What has changed and what stays the same? Look for key differences and similarities. We can get locked into our own worldview and assume that our values are universal. By getting outside of them, we can gain a new perspective that will help us better assess those values.

2. You become the emperor of a small country and have absolute power (let's gloss over the dubious means of how you came by this feat ...). What changes would you make? What laws would you implement or overturn? I'm sure you already have a list, but pick one or two policies that you consider the most important. Is it possible for political legislation to improve a country's 'virtue'?

Would compulsory military service make everyone more courageous; free university education make everyone wiser? We are often tempted to think that change must be implemented from outside. But real change must come from within. And the power to effect that in others is beyond all of us. All we can do is give them the opportunity. Reflect which – if any – of your changes recognize this.

3. Are you a good neighbour? A thoughtful friend? An engaged citizen? What would these things mean in terms of your daily life? How much of your life is taken up thinking only about yourself and your immediate family? Whether your focus is global or local, think of the last time you did something for someone outside of your inner circle, and which didn't involve obligation or getting paid. List things you might do – from small chores to deep commitments – and do them. This may range from being a good friend and giving to charitable causes, to helping your elderly neighbour put out the bins. If the Stoics are right, then such actions form a natural part of our character, and exercising our benevolence and public spiritedness is a means to living a happy, moral life. Take a moment to reflect on what activities of this sort you currently engage in. How do those actions benefit others? Could you do more?

DEATH

WHY YOU'LL NEVER LIVE FOREVER,
AND WHY THAT DOESN'T MATTER

12

Most of us try to avoid thinking about death.

Which is understandable. News of other people's demise is usually upsetting, to whatever degree, based on how close we were to them; and whether we are religious or not, thought of our own demise generally fills us with dread or anxiety – so much stuff left undone, so many people and things we would miss. And all so ... final. What can we do about it?

Well, if you have been following any of the recent technological advances in the field of Transhumanism, then you will see that there are now a promising number of avenues that offer hope that we might yet sidestep the one great inevitability – or at least delay it a good while longer. Developments in genetics and nutrition claim to provide life extension; treatments that help maintain and improve our cognitive and physical functioning beyond the norm. There are even more outlandish technological possibilities that suggest we could have our brains scanned and uploaded to computers, then downloaded into robot bodies, or even freshly 'printed' biological clones of our old self (well, perhaps with a little nip and tuck here and there – why not?). And of course, while we wait for all this to happen, we can just freeze our near-death selves in cryogenic suspension until such a time when technology can defrost and cure us of whatever was about to kill us.

All of which could not be further from any advice that you might get from Stoicism.

As we noted earlier, the Stoics largely agreed with Epicurus that death is the end (see page 88). What little afterlife there might be would be relatively short-lived, after which – to quote Wordsworth – we would return to nature, 'Roll'd round in earth's diurnal course, With rocks, and stones, and trees' ('A Slumber did my Spirit Seal'). Or, as the traditional Yorkshire folk song 'On Ilkla Mooar Baht 'at' more prosaically (and disturbingly) puts it, after you die:

Then the worms will come and eat thee up
Then the ducks will come and eat up the worms
Then we shall come and eat up the ducks
Then we shall have eaten thee

This seems like poor consolation. And in fact, the Stoics' lack of a clear concept of an afterlife was perhaps one factor in its eventual decline in popularity, to be replaced

'You have gone aboard, made your voyage, come to harbour. Disembark: if into another life, there will be God also; if into nothingness, at least you will have done with bearing pain and pleasure, and with your slavery to this vessel so much meaner than its slave. For the soul is intelligence and deity, the body dust and corruption.'

Marcus Aurelius, *Meditations*, III, 3

Here Marcus compares life to a sea voyage: we are born (board ship), live (sail the oceans) and die (arrive at our destination). It is the natural end to our journey and – as he notes elsewhere (II, 17) – 'nothing natural can be evil'. So why do we fear it? Either there is an afterlife – in which case, that too will be ordered by the benign force embodied in Nature – or else you will cease to exist, all sensation will simply end, and with it your mind's slavery to the body, with all its pain and suffering. It's win–win!

by Christianity and Platonism, which were both more optimistic on that front.

However, there *is* consolation there if you look for it. As Epicurus argues (and the Stoics agreed), even if we do not exist after death, this means that there is nothing to fear, for there is nothing left to fear *with*. You will simply not exist. For what we really fear is the *experience* of dying, the thought of the loss of loved ones or some post-mortem state of suffering. In that case, death is like sleep, that nightly period of unconsciousness that we enter into without any such trepidation (dreaming aside, of course, but that's a small part of our nighttime experience – if we even remember it).

If death is nothing to be feared, then that fact should give us more courage to live a moral life. The history of Stoicism is full of such examples – not only of those who took reassurance from death's inevitability to face danger and adversity, or to speak out when it was more prudent to stay silent, but also of those who chose to end their lives voluntarily, calmly and on their own terms.

Some cultures and times have seen suicide as shameful, a sin or an act of weakness. The tide on this is slowly turning, but even now there is still great controversy as to the permissibility of legally assisted suicide for those suffering from unbearable chronic illness. Classical thought was more open to the possibility, usually as a last resort, but for the Stoics suicide could also be an honourable thing. Having been falsely implicated in a plot to kill Nero, the emperor ordered Seneca to take his own life, which – after attending to some correspondence – he calmly did. In the civil war that split apart the Roman Republic, the forces of Cato the Younger had eventually succumbed to those of Julius Caesar (100–44 BC). Deciding that he preferred to die as a free man than to live under the rule of his adversary, Cato stabbed himself in the stomach with his own sword. Neither of these deaths were easy. Having first slit his wrists, Seneca's age and ill health meant that his blood was slow moving, and he had to hasten the end with poison and a hot bath. Cato's friends rushed to his aid and attempted to tend to his wounds, so he tore them back open with his own hands. But both men were rationally convinced in the rightness of their actions.

In addition to the examples of Cato and Seneca, of course, we have Zeno himself, who one day tripped and broke his toe. Taking this as a sign that the earth 'wanted him back', he promptly held his breath until he died. Chrysippus allegedly died laughing from the sight of a donkey eating figs, and after recovering from an illness through fasting, Cleanthes decided to carry on and starve himself to death.

All these incidents emphasize not only the Stoic belief that death is nothing to be feared, but also the idea that, if done at our own time and choosing, it is possible to have a 'good death' (which is the actual meaning of the modern term 'euthanasia'). The Stoics were said to believe that there were five legitimate reasons for suicide: incurable madness or mental deterioration; the suffering of chronic illness; extreme poverty; political oppression that forces us to compromise our moral code; and dying in the defence of one's country or for the performance of some other civic duty (not, strictly speaking, suicide, but there are cases where military

'He who lives longest and he who dies soonest have an equal loss in death. The present moment is all of which either is deprived, since that is all he has. No man can be robbed of that which he has not.'

Marcus Aurelius, *Meditations*, II, 14

We cannot help but think here of the very short lives of Marcus Aurelius's children, only five out of fourteen of whom made it to adulthood, many dying in infancy. Here, we may see him as attempting to console himself that, though it may seem unfair that some die young, the length of a person's life is immaterial, for only the present moment belongs to us – our continuing consciousness. Being robbed of that is the same for everyone. But as for the rest – our possessions, our families, our bodies – none of these things belonged to us in the first place. We cannot lose that which was never ours.

exploits or 'suicide missions' may often entail certain death). But even here Stoics differed among themselves: Marcus Aurelius said that a man who cannot rid himself of vice should contemplate suicide, whereas Epictetus counselled that it is our duty to bear whatever pains God sends us – up to a point (beyond which, it might be considered a hint …).

But the wisdom of accepting the inevitability of death is about more than knowing when to call it a day or choosing when that day will come. The fact that we could die at any time should give us focus, courage and clarity to do the things we want to achieve in the little time we have. Not so much 'eat, drink and be merry, for tomorrow we die' – a phrase often misattributed to Epicurus but actually taken out of context from *The New Testament* (1 Corinthians 15:32) – but rather to remind ourselves of our mortality so that we can motivate ourselves to be more serious and determined, to value those things we have and those people we love while we still have them – but not too much. For the other main Stoic lesson here, remember, is that all things are temporary – your possessions, your abilities, your own life and that of others. We should learn from death to accustom ourselves to that day when the things we value most are no longer there, and by doing so soften the blow.

'Alexander of Macedon and his muleteer, when they died, were in a like condition. They were either alike resumed into the seminal source of all things, or alike dispersed among the atoms.'

Marcus Aurelius, *Meditations*, VI, 24

One last quote from Marcus on death – there are so many good ones, and from the Stoics as a whole. When they died, there was nothing to distinguish the illustrious Alexander the Great from the person who looked after his mules. Both their souls were reabsorbed into the great being that is Nature, and their bodies decayed into their constituent atoms (whether or not this makes Marcus an atomist, like Epicurus, is hard to say – he may only be speaking figuratively). It reminds me of another (I think proverbial) saying, 'When the game is over, both king and pawn go back into the same box'. Death is the great equalizer, but also – Marcus implies – the great revealer: for there is no essential distinction between a great general and a humble mule driver, and all fame is, ultimately, empty.

THINK ABOUT...

There is, as I have mentioned, a common misconception that Stoicism counsels hardheartedness, and that faced with grief, suffering or misfortune, we should simply 'suck it up' and maintain a 'stiff upper lip'. But this is more a caricature of the upper-class Victorian gentleman than a true picture of the Stoic sage, for what the Stoics attempted instead was to see death clearly, as something that none of us can avoid.

Marcus Aurelius lost numerous children, close friends and family, and much of the *Meditations* can perhaps be seen as his attempt to come to terms with this. Seneca, whose life was not devoid of similar grief and suffering, is now famous for his letters to others, counselling them on how to deal with the loss of loved ones. In his letter to Marcia, a woman who had just lost her son, he consoles through philosophy, advising that she focus on death's inevitability, and that even though it seems unjust that a child should predecease its parent, we must remind ourselves that everything that lives is mortal and there are no guarantees of longevity. In another letter, to a father grieving a son, he adopts more practical terms, suggesting that he distract himself from the worst of the pain by throwing himself into his work.

The main thing, for the Stoics, was not to dwell on things, for this would only inflame the passion of grief, thus robbing us of that which is best suited to give us meaningful consolation: our reason. And so, Stoics practised 'premeditations of death', so that through philosophy, a proper understanding of the temporary nature of life

'Never say of anything, "I have lost it", but, "I have restored it". Has your child died? It is restored. Has your wife died? She is restored. Has your estate been taken away? That likewise is restored. "But it was a bad man who took it." What is it to you by whose hands he who gave it has demanded it again? While he permits you to possess it, hold it as something not your own, as do travellers at an inn.'

Epictetus, *Enchiridion*, XI

All that we value is only on loan to us. We are renting it from Nature. What does it matter *how* Nature asks for it back? It makes no difference. This is a hard lesson to take because the experience of grief is so crippling – but no less true, for all that.

'I am endeavouring to live every day as if it were a complete life.'

Seneca, *Moral Letters to Lucilius*, LXI,
"On Meeting Death Cheerfully", 1

We will give the last word to Seneca. Here he is in retirement, during the last few years of his life, writing again to his friend Lucilius. Perhaps he had some forewarning that Nero would soon call for his death, or perhaps he is just an old man whose thoughts have come to dwell on the one approaching inevitability. And of course, he's a Stoic philosopher, from whose mind death is never far. But he is determined to be cheerful, and to be grateful for the life he has. The fact it must come to an end need not be a cause of sadness, and by accepting what we cannot change, we make it easier – for, as he later puts it, 'he who takes his orders gladly, escapes the bitterest part of slavery'. So, even while composing the letter, he lives 'as if death were about to call me away in the very act of writing'. He is not thinking of tomorrow, only of today, of the present, which may end – as it must – at any moment. But that's OK. It is only the 'now' that we have anyway – and that was never really ours to begin with.

and what little control we have over our own or others' well-being, we may come to accept what is inevitable. So rather than 'do not cry', the Stoic's advice is 'do not cry *too much*'. It is natural to grieve, to feel pain and loss, but beyond a certain point – to wallow in our own misery – it will only make things worse.

Is this hard advice? Well, yes. Because it can be hard in the midst of bereavement to retain our mental composure. That doesn't mean that we should bottle it all up in an attempt to repress our grief at all costs, as if there is some shame attached to public displays of emotion.

If you have lost someone, then you will understand that grief can be a strange thing, and people react differently. Those who are visibly emotionally distraught may be seen as being more 'genuine' in their feelings, or having had a closer relationship with the deceased. But this is not necessarily the case, and the quietest – those who muddle through by throwing themselves into practicalities, dwelling upon the choice of coffin linings and the food served at the wake – may be those who suffer most deeply. In terms of outward show, then, there is no 'right' way to grieve, and the Stoic is not really concerned about that. Rather, they want us to look for strength in the one place that may give us true consolation. For the Stoics, that place is not in emotion, but rational reassurance. Death is a factual inevitability, and may come at any time, but it is something for which we can prepare ourselves by remembering that – as Marcus Aurelius says – 'no man can be robbed of that which he has not'.

GOING FURTHER...

1. You are going to die at midnight tonight. How do you feel? Panicked? Scared? Full of regrets? This is normal. But what would be your biggest regret? Make a list (fittingly, the last one I'll ask you to do ...). What things left undone or unsaid would bother you the most? Can you still do or say them? The point is not to create a last-minute bucket list, but to get you to value the present moment. Everything you will lose in death is not in your future or your past but in your possession right now. Make the most of it.

2. Do a web search for 'famous last words'. They're quite a mixed bag, aren't they? Funny, profound, irreverent, tragic, heroic. Maybe copy down those that you find particularly meaningful or entertaining into your Stoic notebook. Now have a think: what would yours be? Or, what would your ideal situation be? What, for you, would be 'a good death'? Does it matter to you? Is there anything you might take from these thoughts that you could use, going forward, that might change your attitude to how you live now?

3. Take a walk through a graveyard. Look at the stories carved there: the long-lived, the lives barely begun; the spouses buried together, who died within months of each other, or the ones buried apart; the ornate and impressive

monuments, graced with verse and epigrams, or the simple headstones, humble and unadorned. In my favourite graveyard (not, you know, that I have a top ten ...) there is an enormous yew tree. The roots are numerous and join up with the massive trunk in a way that makes it seem like the whole tree is made up of countless smaller, separate trees. I often think on that.

NOTES

As mentioned earlier, I've provided the following blank pages for you to make notes as you read through the book. At some point you may want to invest in your own journal for this purpose, but for now feel free to use this space to complete the various exercises, lists, or just to jot down your own ideas, questions or favourite quotes.

_____

_____

_____

_____

_____

_____

_____

_____

_____

_____

_____

_____

EVERYDAY STOICISM

FURTHER READING

If you want to learn more about Stoic philosophy, there is a wealth of popular books out there, so I'll just mention a few:

- *Lives of the Stoics: The Art of Living from Zeno to Marcus Aurelius* by Ryan Holiday and Stephen Hanselman (Profile Books, 2020) is a lively and accessible account of Stoicism using anecdotes drawn from the lives of famous (and not so famous) Stoics. Holiday is a dedicated popularizer of Stoic philosophy and has written a range of other books that are also well worth investigating.
- Massimo Pigliucci is a professional philosopher who also writes on Stoicism for a popular readership; you should definitely check out *How To Be a Stoic: Ancient Wisdom for Modern Living* (Rider, 2017), which strikes a nicely personal tone.
- John Sellars is another philosopher and a founder member of Modern Stoicism, which runs Stoic Week (see below). See his *Lessons in Stoicism: What Ancient Philosophers Teach Us About How to Live* (Penguin, 2020), *Stoicism* (Routledge, 2006) and – for a little 'taste' of the Stoic's main competition – *The Fourfold Remedy: Epicurus and the Art of Happiness* (Penguin, 2022).

There are also lots of online resources:

- Modern Stoicism (**modernstoicism.com**) is a non-profit company of volunteers that publishes articles and runs courses that look to help people apply Stoic philosophy to their lives.

- The Daily Stoic (**dailystoic.com**) is a website, newsletter and podcast run by Ryan Holiday which offers guides, resources and exercises that subscribers can utilize in everyday situations.
- Stoic Week is a yearly event organized by the University of Exeter that invites people to 'live like a Stoic' for seven days. Why not give it a go? See more here: **modernstoicism.com/stoic-week**.

And, of course, there are the writings of the Stoics themselves, all of which are readable and accessible, and available in various modern translations, so I won't specify which. The main texts are:

- Marcus Aurelius: *Meditations*, which was his own private 'journal' for a number of years.
- Epictetus: The *Enchiridion* (his 'handbook', which is very short and concise) and his *Discourses*, which is longer and records his answers to his students on various personal questions. Both books are summaries of Epictetus's lectures compiled by his student Arrian.
- Seneca the Younger: He was the most prolific writer among the Stoics (at least, of those whose work survives) and there are lots to choose from. *Moral Letters to Lucilius*, which collects his correspondence near the end of his life, is a good place to start. Also worth checking out are the *Consolations* (letters to Helvia, his mother, among others), the treatises *On Anger* and *On Benefits*, and the essay *On the Shortness of Life.*

SOURCES

In writing this book, I am indebted to a range of popular and academic texts, first- and second-hand sources. However, I should particularly mention the following, which informed my understanding of some of the finer points of Stoicism and Roman history, and the philosophy of that period (most philosophers' dates are from the *Concise Routledge Encyclopaedia of Philosophy*):

- Ahonen, Marke, 'Ancient Philosophers on Mental Illness', *History of Psychiatry,* 30(1) (2019), 83–100.
- Beard, Mary, *Emperor of Rome* (London: Profile Books, 2023).
- Craig, E, ed., *Concise Routledge Encyclopaedia of Philosophy* (London: Routledge, 1999).
- Long, AA, 'Soul and Body in Stoicism', *Phronesis*, 27(1) (1982), 34–57.
- Rist, JM, *Stoic Philosophy* (Cambridge: Cambridge University Press, 1969).
- Sandbach, FH, *The Stoics* (London: Chatto & Windus, 1975).
- Suetonius, *The Twelve Caesars*, tr. Robert Graves (London: Penguin Books, 1957).

All quotations are taken from public domain translations. These are:

- Cicero, *On the Nature of the Gods*, tr. Francis Brooks (London: Methuen, 1896).
- Diogenes Laërtius, *The Lives and Opinions of Eminent Philosophers*, tr. Charles D. Yonge (London: G. Bell & Sons, 1915).
- *The Discourses of Epictetus; with the Encheiridion and Fragments*, tr. George Long (London: G. Bell & Sons, 1877).
- Epictetus, *Enchiridion*, tr. Thomas W. Higginson (New York: The Liberal Arts Press, 1955).
- King James Bible (Bible Gateway, 2017). Retrieved 12 April, 2024, from www.biblegateway.com/versions/King-James-Version-KJV-Bible
- *The Meditations of the Emperor Marcus Aurelius Antoninus*, tr. George W. Chrystal (Edinburgh: Otto Schulze & Company, 1902).
- Seneca the Younger, *Minor Dialogues*, tr. Aubrey Stewart (London: G. Bell & Sons, 1889).
- *Political fragments of Archytas, Charondas, Zaleucus, and other ancient Pythagoreans, preserved by Stobaeus; and also, Ethical fragments of Hierocles, the celebrated commentator on the Golden Pythagoric Verses, preserved by the same author*, tr. Thomas Taylor (Chiswick: C. Whittingham, 1822).
- Seneca the Younger, *Moral Letters to Lucilius* (3 vols), tr. RM Gummere, (London: Richard Heinmann, 1917–1925).
- Seneca the Younger, *On Benefits*, tr. Aubrey Stewart (London: G. Bell & Sons, 1887).

INDEX

Italics represent quoted material

ABOUT THE AUTHOR

Gareth Southwell is a writer, illustrator and philosopher who lives in South Wales in the UK. He's been involved with philosophy for over thirty years, as a student, teacher, examiner and author. Gareth has published numerous books on various philosophical topics, from Friedrich Nietzsche to René Descartes, political philosophy to the philosophy of science. He is also the author of various works of science fiction. You can sign up to follow his weekly musings at **garethsouthwell.com**.

ACKNOWLEDGEMENTS

My thanks to everyone at Greenfinch for their hard work on this book. To Emily Arbis, for the opportunity to write it, and for her flexibility in accommodating my ideas and suggestions. To Philippa Wilkinson, for her exceptional diligence and skill in helping my words make some sort of sense. To Katie Crous for her meticulous proofread, and to James Pople for his wonderful design. And to Dr Mark, for his Suetonius!

And lastly, as always, to my family, for their love and support, and to whom I am far from indifferent.

First published in Great Britain in 2024 by

Greenfinch
An imprint of Quercus Editions Ltd
Carmelite House
50 Victoria Embankment
London EC4Y 0DZ

An Hachette UK company

A CIP catalogue record for this book is available from the British Library

HB ISBN 978-1-52943-933-5
Ebook ISBN 978-1-52943-934-2

10 9 8 7 6 5 4 3 2 1

Design by James Pople

Printed and bound in India by Manipal Technologies Limited

Papers used by Greenfinch are from well-managed forests and other responsible sources.

MIX
Paper | Supporting
responsible forestry
FSC
www.fsc.org
FSC™ C104740